Passing the
Literacy
Skills Test

Passing the
Literacy
Skills Test

4th Edition

Jim Johnson
Bruce Bond

 SAGE | LearningMatters

Los Angeles | London | New Delhi
Singapore | Washington DC

Learning Matters
An imprint of SAGE Publications Ltd
1 Oliver's Yard
55 City Road
London EC1Y 1SP

SAGE Publications Inc.
2455 Teller Road
Thousand Oaks, California 91320

SAGE Publications India Pvt Ltd
B 1/I 1 Mohan Cooperative Industrial Area
Mathura Road
New Delhi 110 044

SAGE Publications Asia-Pacific Pte Ltd
3 Church Street
#10-04 Samsung Hub
Singapore 049483

Editor: Amy Thornton
Production controller: Chris Marke
Project management: Deer Park Productions
Marketing manager: Lorna Patkai
Cover design: Wendy Scott
Typeset by: C&M Digitals (P) Ltd, Chennai, India
Printed and bound in Great Britain by Henry Ling
Limited at The Dorset Press, Dorchester DT1 1HD

© 2015 Jim Johnson and Bruce Bond

First published in 2001 by Learning Matters Ltd

Reprinted in 2001, 2002, 2003 (twice), 2004, 2005
(twice), 2006 and 2007 (twice). Second edition
published in 2008. Reprinted in 2009 (twice).
Reprinted in 2010. Third edition published in 2012.

Fourth edition published in 2015.

Library of Congress Control Number: 2014956108

British Library Cataloguing in Publication data

A catalogue record for this book is available from
the British Library.

ISBN 978-1-4739-1342-4
ISBN 978-1-4739-1343-1 (pbk)

At SAGE we take sustainability seriously. Most of our products are printed in the UK using FSC papers and boards.
When we print overseas we ensure sustainable papers are used as measured by the Egmont grading system.
We undertake an annual audit to monitor our sustainability.

Contents

Acknowledgements

The publishers would like to thank the TA for permission to use the audio icon on page 2. This was taken from the practice Literacy Skills Test on the TA website www.education.gov. uk and is the copyright of the Teaching Agency.

About the authors

Jim Johnson is an Honorary Fellow of Nottingham Trent University where, until his retirement, he led the English team in the Department of Education.

Working as a member of the AlphaPlus Consultancy team, **Bruce Bond** has worked for over ten years authoring and editing the QTS Literacy Skills Tests. He was also associated with the development and evaluation of the Initial Teacher Training Pilot. He has taught English in the primary, secondary and further education sectors for over 30 years.

Series introduction

The QTS skills test

All new entrants to the teaching profession in England, including those on initial teacher training (ITT) and Graduate Teacher programmes (GTP), have to pass the skills tests to be eligible for the award of qualified teacher status (QTS).

Since September 2013, all trainee teachers have been required to pass these now pre-entry skills tests in numeracy and literacy before starting their course. The pass mark for these tests was raised in September 2013 and the number of re-sits allowed is two.

The tests cover skills in:

- numeracy;
- literacy.

Passing the tests will demonstrate that you can apply these skills to the degree necessary for their use in your day-to-day work in a school, rather than the subject knowledge required for teaching. The tests are taken online by booking a time at a specified centre, are marked instantly and your result, along with feedback on that result, will be given to you before you leave the centre.

You can find more information about the skills tests and the specified centres on the Department for Education's website: www.education.gov.uk/get-into-teaching/apply-for-teacher-training/skills-tests

Titles in this series

This series of books is designed to help you become familiar with the skills you will need to pass the tests and to practise questions on each of the topic areas to be tested.

Passing the Numeracy Skills Test (sixth edition)
Mark Patmore
ISBN 978 1 4739 1175 8 (pbk)
ISBN 978 1 4739 1174 1 (hbk)

Passing the Literacy Skills Test (fourth edition)
Jim Johnson and Bruce Bond
ISBN 978 1 4739 1343 1
ISBN 978 1 4739 1342 4 (hbk)

Introduction

You need to pass a test of your own literacy skills before you can be admitted to a course of teacher education. This applies to all candidates, whether you see yourselves as having an English specialism or not. This book is designed to help you to pass that test. The necessary knowledge is explained, examples of questions are provided and answers to those questions are supplied, along with *Key points* to indicate the main things that need attention.

The areas covered in the book – spelling, punctuation, grammar and comprehension – are the ones that appear in the test. The particular aspects of spelling, etc., are also the ones that are in the test. The actual form of the questions is also similar. Everything you will be tested on is explained; examples are given and the questions give you plenty of practice for the test. The questions in the test will be a selection from the types of question shown here in each section.

Why is the knowledge of English of intending teachers being tested?

Teachers need to have a confident knowledge of English. A teacher who has a sound idea of how the English language is organised can help children to use it well. Some approaches – especially guided writing – can only be successful if the teacher knows, for example, what it is about a child's writing that makes it good and also knows how it could be improved.

Teachers receive a great deal of written information and have to be able to understand it and act on it with assurance. They often have to write, or collaborate in writing, documents such as school policies, reports on their children, information for parents, etc.

Teachers and their use of English are very much in the public eye. Parents, governors, inspectors and others see them in their professional role and, inevitably, make judgements. Teachers need to know enough and be competent enough to deal confidently with the world they move in.

Finally, the right of children to be taught by somebody who knows enough about English to be able to help them is the basis of the test and of this book.

What is the test like?

The test will be carried out online. For the spelling test, you will use headphones (multiple-choice spelling options will be available for candidates with hearing impairment). The test has four sections: Spelling, Punctuation, Grammar and Comprehension.

You will be asked to:

- type in or select your answers for Spelling;
- type in or delete and amend characters for Punctuation;
- drag and drop multiple-choice options into text for Grammar;
- drag and drop options in order to: match statements to categories; complete a list; sequence information; identify points; match text to summaries; identify meaning of words/phrases; evaluate statements; select headings; and identify readership for Comprehension.

You will not be tested on the National Curriculum nor on how to teach English. You will be tested on four main sections of knowledge about literacy: spelling, punctuation, grammar and comprehension.

The spelling section of the test *has* to be attempted first. Once the spelling section is done, you must go on to the other sections and cannot return to spelling. There is no restriction on how you go about the other three sections. You can do them in any order; tackle questions within each section in any order; and move about within each section as much as you like. It may make more sense to do the grammar test last but that is up to you.

In the literacy skills test, each test has a unique pass mark, dependent on the questions that are included. The total number of marks available for each test varies from 45 to 49, again dependent on the questions that are included. Spelling has a total of 10 marks, Punctuation 15, Grammar 10–12 and Comprehension 10–12. If, as is likely, the test has 48 questions, 31 correct answers can gain you a pass.

This is what the four sections cover and how they are approached in the test:

Spelling

Teachers are expected to spell correctly. That includes the words that are likely to appear in their professional work. The emphasis on correct spelling is justified because it avoids ambiguity (for example, advise/ advice; affect/effect) and is easier to read than incorrect spelling. In the test, you are expected to use British English spelling but either *-ize* or *-ise* verb endings will be allowed.

You will need to wear headphones for this part of the real test. You will see ten sentences on the screen. One word has been deleted from each sentence. Where a word has been deleted, there appears an icon for *Audio* 🔊. When you reach that word in your reading, click the icon and listen through your headphones. You will hear the deleted word. Decide how you think it is spelled and type your decision directly into the box provided in the deletion space. If you need to have the word repeated, click the audio icon again. You can do this as many times as you want, even if you are only part of the way through spelling the word, or have finished and just want to check. You may also make several attempts to spell a word but you should keep in mind that the whole test allows only about 45 minutes.

A multiple-choice spelling option is available for candidates with hearing impairment. As this is a book, not a computer, the practice questions follow the same' rubric and format as the hearing impaired multiple-choice questions in the Literacy Skills Test:

Select the correctly spelled word from the box of alternatives. Write your answer in the space in the sentence.

1 As I had used the school's petty cash to buy some materials, I kept all the _____ to give to the head.

> receipts
> receits
> reciepts
> reciets

2 Teachers used their _____ judgement when selecting topics for discussion.

> professional
> proffesional
> profesional
> professionel

Punctuation

Teachers are expected to be able to read and use punctuation correctly, especially in those texts that they are likely to encounter or to produce as part of their professional work. Punctuation that is consistent and that follows the conventions makes a text easy to read. Errors in punctuation not only give a reader more work to do but can also change the meaning or create ambiguity in the text. They can also create a bad impression, especially if the error is caused through obvious carelessness. Knowing what punctuation is needed, and where it should go, reveals both an awareness of the reader's needs and, fundamentally, a high degree of literacy.

Unlike spelling, there is a personal element in punctuation. By the time you have finished the book, you might have noticed that we use more semicolons than most people. Many writers never use semicolons at all. The point is that, if they are used, they should be used consistently.

The point about consistency is such a key one that it is worth considering it here. Suppose you have written this sentence:

My early experience with the class has led me to modify my medium-term plans.

Now suppose that you want to add something to that sentence to express, however mildly, your feelings about having to make the changes. You decide to add the word *unfortunately*. That word can go at the beginning of the sentence (with a comma immediately after it) or at the end (with a comma immediately before it) or in the middle, between *me* and *to*. That is an interruption in the grammatical structure of the sentence and such interruptions are marked by commas. A common failing is to put just one comma, either before or after the interruption, but you actually need two, one before and one after the interruption, like this:

My early experience with the class has led me, unfortunately, to modify my medium-term plans.

Consistency means that you do not put just one comma in this case but that you use both. They are partners.

The test is presented online. You will see a text that has some punctuation omitted. Your task is to identify where to place a punctuation mark, change a lower case letter to an upper case one or create a new paragraph. When you have decided what change to make, double click on the word you have chosen to edit – the word before the punctuation mark – and a dialogue box will appear. The word you clicked will appear in a box. Type in your punctuation and click OK. The box will disappear and the word and your punctuation choice will appear in the text but will now be blue. To add a new paragraph, double click on the word before the new paragraph is to begin, click on the letter 'P' which is in the dialogue box and click OK. You can change your answer if you think you should.

Sometimes, although it is possible to insert a punctuation mark, it may not be necessary or even appropriate. You have to decide. What is very important is that you create a text whose punctuation is wholly consistent. Your criterion is to ask yourself what would be *consistent with the punctuation in the text.* Remember to add up your changes so that they total 15 and also remember there are only 15 correct amendments. If you insert punctuation where it is correct but not necessary, it will not add to your score nor will any marks be deducted.

This is the sort of question you are likely to meet in the book. As this is a book, not a computer, you cannot type in your chosen punctuation mark; instead, you simply note which punctuation mark or other change in punctuation is necessary at which point to make the whole consistent. There will be passages like this for you to practise your knowledge of punctuation; your job is to make it appropriate and consistent in its use of punctuation:

> *although the literacy framework had been working well some staff wondered how to maintain the good work they had done in other areas of the curriculum could drama and pe be retained at the same level as previously*

Grammar

Teachers need to be able to see whether a piece of writing is, or is not, in Standard English, the variety of English that is required in formal texts and, therefore, in almost all writing. They also need to be able to say if the text makes sense and, if not, what prevents it from making sense. Finally, they need to be aware of the style that is appropriate to a particular type of text and to understand what, if anything, is wrong with the style.

The test is multiple-choice. You will see a passage that is not quite complete; bits of language are missing. The decision about what should be inserted to complete the passage is a grammatical choice. You will be shown a range of possible bits of language to insert, only one of which would complete that part of the passage satisfactorily. The choice of that insertion will depend on your reading the whole passage carefully as well as the sentence that has to be completed. You insert your choice simply by dragging it into position.

Below is an example of a sentence that is incomplete. Four possible ways of completing the sentence are offered. Your task is to choose the one that fits grammatically:

The assembly focussed on the current playground incidents

Now choose one of the following to complete the sentence:

a. *that were making life difficult for the infants.*
b. *that was making life difficult for the infants.*
c. *that are making life difficult for the infants.*
d. *that is making life difficult for the infants.*

Comprehension

Teachers receive a good deal of written material that they must understand and to which they must respond. This test puts an emphasis on close, analytical reading of a passage of text. You will need to read the passage with attention to the main ideas, with an awareness of its arguments and, sometimes, with an idea of how it affects your existing ideas. You might need to make judgements about the text and to organise and reorganise its content. Since that is what being a teacher now involves, the test assesses your ability to read in this way.

The comprehension test uses a range of multiple-choice style questions. You will be expected to drag and drop selected options in order to:

- **match statements to categories;**
- **complete a list;**
- **sequence information;**
- **identify points;**
- **match text to summaries;**
- **identify meaning of words/phrases;**
- **evaluate statements;**
- **select headings;**
- **identify readership.**

The test will present you with the sorts of text that teachers are likely to see and read as part of their professional lives. You will be expected to identify key points, read between the lines, tell fact from fiction, make judgements, etc. Not every test will examine every aspect!

At its simplest, the test might ask you to identify the meaning of words and phrases. Remember that no one test will test every aspect of every one of the four sections. In the following short passage, for example, you are asked to identify from a given list of options who you think is the intended audience for the text:

You will have seen from the local press, where results are published from every school in the Authority, that this school has had a consistently high standard of performance in the annual SATs over several years. This fine record is expected to continue for some years, at least. A consequence of this success is that the school is oversubscribed each year and, regretfully, it is not always possible to offer a place to every child whose parents apply to us.

How to prepare for the test

- Use this book to get a good grasp of what understanding is demanded by the test.
- Go to the DfE website (www.education.gov.uk/sta/professional/b00211208/literacy) to read their advice, familiarise yourself with the test and what it looks like, and try the practice tests.
- From that practice, identify which areas you need to improve on and refer to this book.
- Remember that doing well in spelling and punctuation can take you close to the pass mark.
- Read again the Hints in each section of this book.

How to use this book

For the purposes of the test, literacy is seen as comprising the four sections detailed above: Spelling, Punctuation, Grammar and Comprehension. Each section has its own chapter. There you will find an explanation of the knowledge required, examples of the features of literacy being tested and explicit direction about what to do in the test. There are practice questions for each section.

Chapter 5 is a complete literacy practice skills test for you to work through, and Chapter 6 contains answers and explanatory key points for all the questions in the main chapters, and for the practice test.

Revision checklist

The following chart shows in detail the coverage of the four main chapters. You can use the checklist in your revision to make sure that you have covered all the key content areas.

SPELLING	Pages
Spelling questions will cover the main spelling rules and include words used by people involved in teaching.	8–21
PUNCTUATION	
Paragraphing	22–23
Full stop	23
Commas	23
Colon	26
Semicolon	26
Question mark	26
Brackets/parentheses	27
Speech marks	27
Quotation marks	27
Hyphens	28
Apostrophes	28–30
Capital letters	30

1 | Spelling

Introduction

10 marks are available for spelling.

If you want to write well, good spelling is not as important as good grammar or even good punctuation but it is still important. Some great writers have been poor spellers; some bad writers can spell any word they need.

Correct spelling is not a mark of intelligence but it is very helpful to a reader because poor spelling interferes with the flow of easy reading. If a text is correctly written, the good spellings will not be noticed because all the reader's attention has gone straight to the meaning. Ideally, when someone reads what you write, they should be able to pay attention to what you want to say, to your meaning, and not be distracted by poor spelling. Bad spelling interferes with the reader's attention just as a fault in glass can interfere with the view through a window.

There are no tricks in the test; you will not have to learn how to spell *phthisis* especially for the occasion. If you can spell the kinds of word that are in common use, especially in the world of education, you will have no problems. British spelling rather than American is expected although either *-ise* or *-ize* at the ends of some verbs is acceptable. However, be consistent in your use of whichever you choose.

The actual form of the test is described in the Introduction. For the Literacy Skills Practice Test in Chapter 5, you will be given ten short sentences. One word has been deleted from each sentence. A box below the sentence contains four alternative spellings of the missing word. Complete the sentence by writing in the correct spelling of the missing word.

Essential knowledge

The commonest spelling problem for adults, even educated and well-read adults, is when to use a **double consonant,** as in:

accommodation	*exaggerate*	*harass*
committee	*success*	*assess*
professional	*apprentice*	*misspell*
disappoint	*innumerable*	

Unfortunately, there is no easy way to remember them. They have to be learned by heart. What does help is simply to write a good deal. If you are in the habit of writing, even brief notes to yourself to help you to think through an issue, all aspects of your writing (with the probable exception of handwriting!) will improve. As with so much in life, use it or lose it.

It does help you if you notice those words that you know give you trouble. Look at the following list of some double-consonant words and copy out any that you suspect have been problems for you in the past. When you have a list, look at each word in turn, remember the *whole word*, its sequences of letters, its prefix and suffix (if any), and try to write it again. Then check it.

abbreviate	*immeasurable*
acclimatise	*(in)efficient*
address	*millennium*
allowed	*miscellaneous*
apparent	*miscellany*
appear	*necessary*
apprentice	*occur/occurred*
approach	*occurrence*
appropriate	*omit/omission*
approve	*opportunity*
approximate	*parallel*
assess	*passage*
challenge	*permissible*
commensurate	*permission*
commit/committed	*possess*
correspondence	*proceed (but precede)*
correspondent	*questionnaire*
curriculum	*recommend*
disappear	*recur/recurrence*
dissipate	*satellite*
embarrass	*succeed*
exaggerate	*success*
excellent	*succinct*
grammar	*terrible*
grip/gripped	*truthfully*
happily	*till (but until)*
harass	*vacillate*

There is a special category of words with double consonants. Some stem words, like *fulfil* in *fulfilling*, end in a single consonant – that is, a vowel and a consonant – but then double the final consonant if either *-ed* or *-ng* is added. Some other words in this category are:

commit   *begin*

Note: Benefit, benefited *are exceptions.*

Remarkably, since spelling is normally either right or wrong, you are allowed two choices for *bias* and *focus*. Both *biassed* and *biased* and both *focussed* and *focused* are acceptable spellings.

> *HINT*   Some spellings just have to be learned. Make a list of your own 'hard words'.

We spell words in English in the way we do for a variety of reasons, such as trying to represent:

- a difference in meaning, despite a similarity in sound – for example, *there, their, they're*;
- related meanings, despite some variation in sound – for example, *medicine, medical, medicinal*;
- an earlier pronunciation – for example, *knight*;
- a foreign origin – for example, *chalet*.

If the way we sound words was the only guide to their spelling, *phonics* might be spelled *fonnix*. Many English Northerners say *look* to rhyme with *spook*; most Southerners rhyme it with the Northern *luck*. But the main reason for spelling words as we do is that they **represent the sounds we speak**. This often seems unlikely but it does account for more spelling features than any other factor. Therefore, it helps to use this when learning some words that are fairly regular phonically.

Some of the words that can be learned like this are:

homophone   pronounce   pronunciation   effect

It can help to see if a word you find hard to spell can be pronounced in a way that reminds you of its spelling. On the other hand, be careful. Some words have the same sound – in the following examples, *e* – but are written differently:

ate   jeopardy   pleasure   said

A few words are often pronounced wrongly. *Mischievous* is sometimes spoken with an *ee* sound before the *-ous* and the speller needs to beware of that influence.

Although the sound/letter correspondence is so important in English, it still needs to be recognised that there are many **homophones**: words that sound alike but do not look alike or mean the same thing.

Learn by heart words that cannot be learned in any other way. One other way, in some cases, might be to invent a mnemonic. The student who wrote:

The children took too my personality.

might have been helped by something like:

Two *days ago, I went* **to** *work despite feeling* **too** *tired to get up.*

Other homophones include:

allot/a lot	*meet/meat/mete*
aloud/allowed	*pare/pear/pair*
ate/eight	*practise/practice*
doe/dough	*read/red*
due/dew	*sore/saw*
hare/hair	*wait/weight*
lead/led	*wear/where*
lent/leant	*wheel/weal*

Incidentally, although students have asked on three occasions for an 'explanation of the difference between *as* with an *h* and *as* without an *h*', this is not strictly a homophone. It is simply a reminder that the way in which any of us speaks is not always a good guide to how words are written.

Some words seem to be easily confused. Students have written:

people off all ages

instead of:

people of all ages.

Some write:

could of

instead of:

could have.

The main reason for this error is that *could have* is often abbreviated in speech to *could've*. The pronunciation of *could've* is almost identical to that of *could of*, which is a spelling error. The pronunciation of *should've, must've, would've*, etc. (the abbreviations of *should have, must have, would have*, etc.) accounts for the frequent spelling confusions of *should of, must of, would of*, etc.

The difference is in meaning in the case of *off* instead of *of* and in grammar in the case of *of* instead of *have*. *Off* is used to mean something like *movement from a position*, as in *jump off, take off, off with his head*. After a modal verb such as *could*, you need another, main, verb such as *have*, not a preposition like *of*.

Some words are best learned by heart, such as either those that look as if, by analogy, they should be spelled like another word you know or those that simply have no analogy. These include such words as:

awe	ladle	rhythm
awful	merit	sceptic
curiosity	mileage	schedule
curious	monotonous	scheme
eighth	naive	separate
fifth	occasion	sixth
half	prestige	suspicion
halves	prevail	table
heroes	prevalent	thorough
humorous	psychiatrist	tried
humour	pursue	try
ideology	queue	twelfth
judgement	repertoire	unanimous
label	rhyme	vicious

Notice that some words have a pattern of letters that is fairly consistent – for example, the four-vowel pattern of a repeated *ue* in *queue*, the *-ous* ending in *humorous*. Some words, like *prevail* and *prevalent*, not only add a morpheme (such as *-ent*) when they become another part of speech but also change the spelling of the stem word (the *i* is dropped from *prevail* as the *u* is dropped from *humour* when it is changed to *humorous*).

Some words are spelled one way when they are nouns and another way when they are verbs:

Noun: *practice*   *advice*   Verb: *practise*   *advise*

If you could say *the* before a word, it is a noun and ends in *-ice*. If you could say *I, you, we, they* before it, it is a verb and ends in *-ise*.

Some long words can be broken down into parts:

miscellany = misc + ell + any

You need to notice the features of each part: the *sc*; the double *ll*; the recognisable word *any.*

Some words can be broken down into smaller words:

weather = w + eat + her   *together = to + get + her*

We confess our indebtedness to a boy aged five for revealing that truth about *together*!

Remember the patterns – the sequences of letters – in words that repeat particular letters:

minimise   *curriculum*   *remember*

Remember is often misspelled, simply because of the crowded repetition of *e* and *m*.

Notice what happens when a **suffix** is added.

Just as *humour* loses its second *u* when it becomes *humorous,* so we find other changes when a word takes a suffix:

To form the plural of a word that ends in *y*, drop the *y* and add *ies*:

fairy   *fairies*   *country*   *countries*

To add *-ed* or *-ing* to a verb that ends in *-e*, drop the *e*:

manage   *managed*   *managing*
create   *created*   *creating*
solve   *solved*   *solving*

To add *-ed* or *-ing* to a verb with a short vowel sound, double the final consonant:

rap   *rapped*

To add *-ed* or *-ing* to a verb with a long vowel sound, keep the final consonant single:

reap   *reaped*

If you can develop a feel for the ways that English words are built, for their **morphology**, it will help you to see where one part ends and another begins. This can help particularly with longer and less common words and with the common affixes:

mis + take   *dis + tinc + tion*   *dis + agree + able*

It is not obvious but the suffix is *-tion,* not *-ion.*

> **HINT** Note that the prefixes *mis* and *dis* end in one *s* only. That helps when you add *dis* to *appear* to make *disappear:* not *dissappear.*

Some words, connected by meaning – and in these cases, therefore, by spelling – vary a little in the way they sound but that has to be ignored:

photo   *photograph*   *photographer*   *photographic*

The letters *sc* represent the *s* sound if the following letter is *e* or *i:*

discipline   *adolescent*   *descent*

On the other hand, they represent the *sk* sound if the following letter is *r, l, a, o, u:*

discrepancy   *discussion*

When do you write *ie* and when do you write *ei*? This rule works:

For the sound *ee,* put *ie* as in:

believe   *mischief*   *niece*

For the sound *ee,* put *e* before *i* when the preceding letter is *c:*

conceive   *deceive*   *receive*

However, this only applies to words where the sound is *ee* and not to words like:

weight   *forfeit*   *friend*

Many people ignore that last part of the rule.

> **HINT**   *i* before *e,* except after *c,* when the sound is *ee.*

Most words that end with the sound in *recent* use *-ent:*

confident	*emergent*	*equivalent*	*excellent*
impatient	*independent*	*prevalent*	*reminiscent*

Very few words use -*ant*:

preponderant   *quadrant*   *redundant*

> **HINT**   Since far more words end in -*ent or -ence*, it pays to focus on and learn any
> that end in -*ant* or -*ance*.

A very common error is to use the wrong letters to represent the vowel sound in *sir*.
Words like these just have to be learned by heart:

*pur*sue   *separate*   **bird**   **word**

The sound *s* is often written with a *c*, especially if the *c* is followed by an *e* or *i*, as in:

concede   *deficit*   *necessary*

Sometimes, it is written with a -*ce*, especially at the end of a word:

practice   *prejudice*

Sometimes, it is written with an *s*, even when it is not expected:

idiosyncrasy   *consensus*   *supersede*

Or with an -*se*:

practise   *premise*

And even with -*sc*:

miscellaneous *miscellany*   *scene*

General tips

Keep a dictionary nearby to check problem words and then try to learn them. Look out for
commonly used letter-strings, for affixes and other morphological features and simply for
anything unusual.

See if you tend to make particular errors, such as not noticing that *separate* has an *a* in
the middle or that *develop*, unlike *envelope*, does not end with an *e*.

Try sounding out. On the whole, words that are phonically regular do not cause spelling
problems but some writers lose their faith in that regularity. Try it.

Look at the whole of a word, not just its individual letters, and try to remember that
whole. If it helps, say the letters to yourself rhythmically.

Look for possible analogies, for example, *eight*, *height* and *weight*.

Pay special attention to the letter-strings in foreign words. Their foreignness includes their combining letters differently from English:

fjord   craic   khaki   macho   graffiti   Pilsner   cha siu

Do not trust the spell check on a word processor. Any spell check will allow *top* when you meant *to*, *were* when you meant *where* and *feather* when you meant *father*. A spell check will correct non-words, like *teh* when the writer intended *the*, but it is still necessary to read through a late draft to check the spelling yourself.

If you know which words you tend to get wrong when you use a word processor *(have* and *because*, in my case!), go to *Tools*, *Autocorrect* and type in both the way you regularly type them (wrongly) and also the correct way. The processor will then automatically correct your spelling. But remember that this does nothing for your own ability to spell!

Questions

In the Literacy Skills Test you will be asked to spell ten words. These will be examples of words that are most likely to be encountered within the professional context of teaching. They represent the vocabulary, and its correct spelling, that fellow professionals, parents and pupils would expect every teacher to know.

All the words below are in general use; some follow generic spelling rules and some are spellings that just have to be learned by heart.

Select the correctly spelled word from the box of alternatives. Write your answer in the space in the sentence.

1. Annie enjoyed doing so much _____ work on her Charlemagne Extended Project Qualification.

   indipendent
   indipendant
   independent
   independant

2. The group had made _____ progress with their task.

   demonstrible
   demonstratable
   demonstrable
   demonstreble

(Continued)

(Continued)

3. Some useful _____ resources can be found on the internet.

asessment

assessmant

assesment

assessment

4. Research shows there is a marked increase in creativity during _____.

adolescence

adolescents

adolesence

adolesensce

5. Pupils were encouraged to _____ their own reading topics.

persue

purrsue

parsue

pursue

6. Most of the class found the _____ in the school's production of *A Midsummer Night's Dream* quite unconvincing.

fairys

faries

fairies

fareys

7. _____ ingredients in Home Economics assessed the pupils' numeracy skills.

Weighting

Wieghing

Weighing

Waying

8. The prospect of visiting the coast _____ the pupils' enthusiasm for the project.

fuelled
feulled
fueled
fuled

9. Some of the pupils were deeply _____ by the contents of the diaries.

effected
afected
efected
affected

10. Two posts offering greater _____ were being advertised in the school.

responsability
responserbility
responsibility
responsebilty

11. Most pupils found the _____ tests *very* helpful.

practise
practiss
practisce
practice

12. The experiment proved that substances do not _____ when they dissolve.

disapear
dissappear
disappear
disappeare

(Continued)

(Continued)

13. Field trip regulations include strict regulations about the _____ of knives.

> possession
> posession
> possesion
> possessions

14. It proved _____ to move the whiteboard just for one meeting.

> impracticible
> unpracticible
> impracticable
> unpracticable

15. The class responded well to the range of _____ poems their teacher presented.

> humouros
> humorous
> humourous
> hummorous

16. The small sample shows how percentages can give an _____ impression.

> exagerated
> exaggarated
> exagarated
> exaggerated

17. _____ the heavy snow meant that the school concert had to be postponed.

> Regretably
> Regrettably
> Regrettebly
> Regreatably

18. Some left-handed pupils _____ write across the page from right to left.

automaticly
autimatically
automaticaly
automatically

19. The conference addressed new approaches to _____ delivery.

curiculum
curriculum
curicullum
curicculum

20. Some pupils may not admit to problems with mathematics due to _____.

embarassment
embarrasment
embarrassment
embarasment

21. Teachers need a sound knowledge of their subject areas and related _____.

pedergogy
pedogogy
pedagogy
pedagogey

22. Pupils are _____ to attend school in casual clothing on Own Clothes Day.

aloud
allowed
alowed
aloued

(Continued)

(Continued)

23. When he came to _____ art materials among the children he was working with, Joe found that he had miscounted.

alot
a lot
alott
allot

24. The junior school choir sang with a _____ that was beyond their age.

maturity
maturaty
matturity
maturety

25. Support and _____ are key parts of the anti-bullying policy.

counciling
counselling
counsiling
councelling

26. What had once seemed a _____ collection of options now seemed very logical.

miscellanious
miscellaneous
missellanious
miscelanious

27. My answer to the question about death rates in Napoleon's army had to be an _____.

aproximation
approximation
approximacion
approcsimacion

28. It was clearly _____ of me to be late for the exam.

> reprehensable
> repprehensable
> repprehensabel
> reprehensible

29. Irina spent weeks discussing whether a degree or an _____ would suit her better.

> apprenticeship
> aprenticeship
> aprentiship
> aprentiseship

2 | Punctuation

Introduction

Fifteen marks are available for punctuation. That is almost halfway to the pass mark.

Punctuation has often been undervalued yet its importance in conveying your meaning to a reader clearly and unambiguously is great. Poor or missing punctuation can lead to the reader getting a quite false impression, as in:

After we left the pupils, the parents and I went to meet the headteacher.

if what you meant was:

After we left, the pupils, the parents and I went to meet the headteacher.

In the second sentence the comma changes the meaning so that it is clear that the pupils also went to meet the headteacher.

A literate teacher may need to check his or her spelling often but is, by definition, able to use punctuation well.

The aspects of punctuation in the test are concerned with ways in which writers mark off *units of meaning* (such as a sentence), ways in which the actual status of the language being used is clarified and ways in which words themselves are punctuated.

The main ways of marking 'units of meaning'

Any text is made up of parts: the whole text, the paragraphs, the sentences, the clauses and the phrases. These are the units of meaning greater than the individual word. The main ways in which we mark off where one unit ends and another begins are:

- paragraph;
- full stop;
- comma.

None of these is straightforward; all are partly a matter of personal style. Consequently, the key is to be consistent with punctuation within any one text.

Paragraphing

A paragraph is a group of one or more sentences that have enough related meaning, enough similarity in content or topic, to form a group. The writer decides where to begin and end each paragraph, depending on how he or she regards the main groups of meaning.

A good text is divided along consistent lines, following the same idea about what makes a chunk of meaning, and one sentence within the paragraph states the main idea. This is the topic sentence; it often comes first.

Good paragraphing also makes considered use of sentence adverbs, those connectives, such as *However*, *Furthermore*, *On the other hand*, *Fortunately*, etc., that link the meaning of the new paragraph to the previous one.

However, the choice of where to start a new paragraph can sometimes be very subjective. The main reason is to show when a writer is:

- **switching to a new idea;**
- **highlighting an important point;**
- **showing a change in time or place;**
- **emphasising a contrast; or**
- **indicating progression toward a summary or conclusion.**

The test might show you a text that could have paragraphs but that is printed without any; you might be asked to identify where paragraph boundaries could come.

> **HINT**   If you are uncertain about inserting a paragraph break, check the number of definite punctuation omissions you have already amended. Remember, there are only 15 unequivocally missing pieces of punctuation. If you have made 14 changes and cannot see another obvious omission, apart from the need for a paragraph break, this is probably the fifteenth instance where punctuation is needed.

Full stop

Full stops define a sentence, literally, by showing its limit. You need to develop a sense of what a sentence is to use full stops properly. If the largest unit of meaning is the unbroken, complete text and the next largest is the paragraph, the largest below that is the sentence. As a rule, it is one or more clauses long, has a sense of relative completeness about it and usually has a verb and its subject.

Over 80 per cent of all the punctuation marks used in British English are full stops and commas.

> **HINT**   To help you to get a better grip of sentences and their need for a final full stop, look at *Clause, Sentence* and *Verb* in the Glossary. Keep that in mind as you read about commas.

Commas

It is not a simple task to use commas well. The first and simplest guidance is:

if you are not sure whether to use a comma or a full stop, use a full stop and begin a new sentence.

It was just what I had been looking for, from my experience with the previous class I felt a need for children who wanted to learn.

should be:

It was just what I had been looking for. From my experience with the previous class, I felt a need for children who wanted to learn.

Commas help us to separate items in a list. They can, therefore, be used as an alternative to the word *and* but not as well as *and*:

Above all, Zeinab likes to teach maths, geography, art and history.

You do not need a comma after *art* because *and* here does the job of a comma. This could be written using *and* instead of a comma:

Above all, Zeinab likes to teach maths and geography and art and history.

Sometimes, we use a phrase or word at the beginning of a sentence and then start to write what we mean.

The sentence above is an example: it begins with *sometimes* and then continues with the subject of the sentence, *we*. Put a comma after that opening word or phrase before continuing with what you want to say. Apart from that *sometimes*, other common **sentence-openers,** or sentence adverbs, are:

On the other hand,
However,
Suddenly,
Next,
Instead,
Unfortunately,

Sometimes, we want to vary what we say by changing the order in which we say things. This might be because we want to *emphasise* something or other:

My last tutor asked if he could copy my maths plans because he felt that they were a good model.

This could be turned round without changing, adding or omitting any words but by adding a comma at the break:

Because he felt that they were a good model, my last tutor asked if he could copy my maths plans.

This is a rather tricky use of the comma. It can be important because it tells the reader precisely what the meaning is. The use of commas can put an end to *ambiguity.* This comma-free sentence is ambiguous:

The teachers who live in Gotham are all over six feet tall.

As it stands, this seems *very* improbable. But suppose the sentence is just about a group of people over six feet who simply happen to live in Gotham. That is more than probable.

The fact that they live in Gotham is almost an afterthought. The essence of the sentence, the main clause, is:

The teachers are all over six feet tall.

Now, an extra, incidental bit of information is given. It is a relative clause:

who live in Gotham

This extra clause can be **embedded** in (set inside) the main clause. To show that it is extra, it is separated from the rest by commas:

The teachers, who live in Gotham, are all over six feet tall.

(This use of the embedded clause is a sophistication that the devisers of the Primary National Strategy wanted to see promoted in schools.)

Not only clauses are embedded. We embed phrases and single words. They may appear at the beginning of a sentence (see the opening sentence adverbs above), in the middle or at the end. Children can be helped by having a discussion about what to embed in a sentence (if anything) and where in the sentence the embedded item might go:

Naturally, the choice of where to apply was rather limited.

or:

The choice of where to apply was rather limited, naturally.

or:

The choice of where to apply was, naturally, rather limited.

The embedded item is bounded by a capital letter and a comma at the beginning of the sentence, by a comma and a full stop at the end and by two, paired commas in the middle.

When we write *dialogue*, a comma ends the text before the quotation marks and the spoken words begin:

Gobinda said, 'Come along with me, children.'

What commas cannot do is end a sentence.

Additional ways of marking 'units of meaning'

These additional ways are the use of:

- **colon;**
- **semicolon;**
- **question mark;**
- **brackets.**

Colon

The commonest use of the colon is to introduce a list:

> *The children brought a wealth of evidence from the playground: sweet wrappers, milk straws, cards to swap, crisp packets and some cigarette packets.*

Another use is to introduce some reasoning or evidence to support the part of the sentence that comes before the colon:

> *Some of them blamed the secondary school children: they reminded the class that several teenagers regularly took a short cut across their playground.*

Semicolon

The semicolon is rarely used in the writing of many people; not only students and teachers but some of our greatest writers ignore this mark. It is possible to write without using it but it can allow a writer to put two independent clauses together that could stand as individual sentences but that the writer feels are unusually closely related. This book contains examples in its text.

Another use of the semicolon is to mark off items in a list following a colon, especially if the items in the list are each several words long:

> *The school still had some problems: a falling roll; two teachers due to retire within the year; an imminent Ofsted inspection.*

However, commas can also do that job. Be careful: if one of those items has so many words that the phrase itself needs a comma, all the items must be separated by a semicolon.

Question mark

This mark ends a sentence that asks a question:

> *Is your personal statement nearly ready?*

> *Will we need supply cover for next Tuesday?*

It is not necessary at the end of a sentence that implies a question but that has the structure of a statement (that is, the subject comes before the verb):

> *I wonder if there will be any supply teachers available.*

> *I asked him when he would be ready for swimming.*

If the sentence is within quotation marks, the question mark comes before the final quotation mark:

> *'Can we get together about this Performance Management meeting?'*

> *'Could you tell me why your assignment is 3,000 words over the limit?'*

Brackets or parentheses

These marks (the two words really mean the same) begin and end an aside in a sentence. Often, a writer composes a sentence but wants to add something to it that is not strictly part of the sentence; rather, it is almost an afterthought or something that he or she would like to say as well as the sentence:

Not many of us (at least, not those under 60) can remember what it was like to teach in those controversial times.

We have had no child statemented (none that we were successful in having statemented, anyway!) for over five years now.

HINT Look at *Parenthesis* in the Glossary.

Punctuation which indicates the status of the language being used

The status of the language being used is shown by the use of:

- **speech marks;**
- **quotation marks.**

Speech marks (double quotes) and quotation marks (single quotes) can help you to make it clear to the reader that this or that piece of your writing is to be read in a particular way. Both can be, and are, in some published texts, used to mark **direct speech,** such as the dialogue in a story.

A teacher might write a story with a class. Any dialogue, words actually spoken by a character, will need to be put inside **speech marks:**

When Fergus the king asked Nes to be his wife, she replied, "Only if I get something in return."

"What is that?" he asked.

Quotation marks can be used for the same purpose but they are valuable in their own right. They can draw the reader's attention to the way that some word or phrase sits oddly in the text as a whole:

When buying travel insurance for their children, parents and carers are advised to be mindful of the so-called 'get out clause' used by some insurance firms.

They help the reader to see that a part of the text actually comes from some source other than the writer:

Song asked his teacher for help with his exposé but was told to 'just get on with it'.

They tell the reader that some of the text is the name of a film or the title of a book:

Shamila started to read 'Harry Potter and the Goblet of Fire' but the spiders scared her so she stopped.

> **HINT** Parentheses, speech marks and quotation marks all work in pairs. If the test shows just one parenthesis or speech/quotation mark, you know that there has to be another. Look for where it might be.

Punctuation within words

The marks that occur within single words are:

- hyphens;
- apostrophes;
- capital letters.

They give the reader information about that word, rather than showing how larger units of meaning are organised or bounded.

Hyphens

Hyphens link two words that have another meaning when they occur together. Some of the first elements are words in themselves, others are abbreviations or suffixes:

well-stocked, ex-headteacher, post-Ofsted, pro-uniform, U-turn, T-shirt

This sort of hyphenated word is a kind of halfway point between two words and one.

Apostrophies

The apostrophe, a minefield for some writers, has two main uses but is sometimes wrongly used for a third purpose.

Abbreviation or omission
When we write, we sometimes choose to leave letters out of words to get closer to the way we speak English. Because we rarely sound the full value of *we will, we do not, we shall not, we cannot*, we may abbreviate them:

we'll, don't, shan't, can't

One of the trickiest of these abbreviations is the use of *it's*, easily confused with *its*. The solution is simply never to write *it's*. *It's* is always an abbreviation, usually of *it is* but sometimes of *it has*. Abbreviations are normal in informal writing but unknown in formal texts. Only use *it's* when you mean to write an informal text and when you mean either *it is* or *it has*:

It's appropriate to write formally.

means the same as:

> *It is appropriate to write formally.*

> *It's become obvious that clear writing matters.*

means the same as:

> *It has become obvious that clear writing matters.*

You will then write *its* only without an apostrophe and only when it is appropriate: as the direct equivalent of *her* or *his* before a noun:

> *The new teaching assistant put down her bag, helped Nathan out of his wheelchair and covered its seat with a cushion.*

Only use the apostrophe as abbreviation when you feel quite confident and in control as a writer.

> **HINT**   Never write *it's*. Write *it is* or *it has* instead and you can forget that apostrophe problem.

Possession
Books have titles. Write down who or what *possesses* the titles:

> *the book*

then put an apostrophe:

> *the book'*

and ask: does this word end with the letter *s*? If not, add one:

> *the book's*

and continue:

> *the book's title.*

If there are several books, you would have the sequence:

> *the books*

then put an apostrophe

> *the books'*

and ask: does this word end with the letter *s*? If it does, leave it alone:

> *the books'*

and continue:

the books' titles.

There is no need to think about singular or plural provided you place the apostrophe before you check if the word ends in s or not. Of course, the way this works means that, in most cases, the placing of the apostrophe does say whether the word before is singular or plural but that does not always help. If men have ambitions and you want to write about that affliction, the singular and plural – *man* and *men* – would look like this:

the man	*the men*
the man'	*the men'*
the man's	*the men's*
the man's ambitions	*the men's ambitions*

The wrong use of the apostrophe plus *s* as a plural form
The sight of cards on market stalls saying *Cabbage's* and *Cauliflower's* (and *Ca'fe* in one town) has led to the rather unfair name of *Greengrocers' Apostrophe* for this wrong use of 's instead of the simple plural's'.

There is a special, and wrong, case of the apostrophe-as-plural that goes far beyond the efforts of any greengrocer. We now have quite a few words in English that end with a vowel, especially o: *video, studio, radio, data, scampi, criteria,* etc. Some people add 's to these words to indicate a plural: *video's,* etc. There is no need. For most of these words, simply add s (the commonest way of making plurals in English). In the case of *data* and *media* and *criteria*, these words are already plural; there is no need to add anything to them at all. However, you can only have one criterion and many criteria and one medium being part of the media.

Capital letters

A capital letter is always needed at the beginning of a new sentence:

Only in my wildest dreams could I have succeeded in obtaining a place on such a course.

It is needed for titles and proper nouns: the names of people and places:

The letter from the Headteacher, Mrs Pendlebury, welcomed me to Ordsall.

There is no need to use a capital for *headteacher* if there is no name to follow.

Questions

Like all the tests, this one is computerised. Details of what you do in the test and how you do it are on page 4, but it will also help you a lot to look at the website http://media.education.gov.uk/assets/files/pdf/l/literacy%20skills%20test%20specification.pdf. If you want to change anything, that can be done. You will not need to delete any punctuation.

The test will present you with a text from which much of the punctuation has been deleted. Your task is to create a properly punctuated complete text from this incomplete one. The key thing, again, is consistency: read the text and its existing punctuation as information about how to complete it. Remember, there are only 15 omissions of punctuation in the test.

The passages below are examples of the kind of test you will have.

Since you are doing this test in a book and not on a computer, read the whole passage and add any punctuation you feel is necessary in pencil or by making a note. Where you want to change a lower case to a capital letter, put a circle round the letter and write *cap* in the margin; where you want a new paragraph, put a forward slash (/) immediately before the first word of the new paragraph and write *np* in the margin.

1. As soon as we speak we reveal a great deal of ourselves to our audience. Suppose you ask someone,

   "shall we have a drink

   Suppose the other person replies

   "Yes, I'd like a whiskey me."

   That tag, *me*, tells you that the speaker probably comes from manchester.

   Sometimes, what people say does tell you something about their origin but it is less definite. A friend asks you and another friend,

   "Now, what would youse two like to drink?"

   The questioner may or may not come from Ireland but will certainly have a background there because that use of youse, unknown in Standard English, has its roots in the Irish having one form of 'you' for one person tú and another form of 'you' for two people sibh. However none of this means that any of these speakers could actually speak any Irish!

2. The concern of the head of english was evident after reading the Can do Better' report on literacy. If we look at boys performance in English, we have to agree that there is, generally some cause for concern. Is there anything that can be done to help them improve?

   Among the short term approaches that seemed to help boys are :
   enthusiastically encouraged private reading;
   clearly set tasks
   explicit teaching of reading strategies;
   a wide range of outcomes from reading;
   reading preferences that are discussed.

3. What is it about Standard English that makes it standard Like every language, English has gone through many changes. The Saxons and Angles who settled here brought their own languages with them predominantly Saxon, and after a while, the dialects of Anglo-Saxon overcame the Celtic languages that had

(Continued)

(Continued)

flourished along with Latin until soon after the Romans left in 410 AD. The languages spoken by the later Scandinavian invaders were probably just about intelligible to some of the Anglo-Saxons but changes and borrowings continued: the new invaders legacy to us includes they, **them, their.** Anglo-Saxon, modified by Scandinavian, with dialects that were barely intelligible to other Anglo-Saxon speakers, continued for hundreds of years but, thankfully it became simpler The German word for **big** is **gross** but it has six versions. Our Anglo-Saxon ancestors had eleven versions of adjectives we have just three: **big, bigger, biggest.** Even when we complicate matters by having **good, better best,** that is still easier than Anglo-Saxon.

Introduction

8–12 marks are available for grammar.

One of the main jobs of a teacher is to work with colleagues in producing documents for a variety of audiences, from known people within the school to outside bodies, and for a range of purposes, from planning teaching to explaining and presenting work that has been done. That collaboration involves drafting, redrafting and proof-reading. This test does not test your writing nor your knowledge of grammatical terms; rather, it will test:

- **your grasp of written Standard English;**
- **your ability to identify and use it unambiguously;**
- **your understanding of which style is appropriate to the text in question.**

How will these three aspects of grammatical knowledge be tested? What, in detail, do those aspects mean you need to know?

The grammar section of the test presents you with two or three short pieces of text. The text is usually an example of the everyday reading or writing material that a teacher might be expected to encounter in the course of their professional duties. Such texts might include:

- **notes or letters to parents and carers;**
- **notes or letters to or from colleagues;**
- **minutes of meetings;**
- **information about training and professional development;**
- **articles for school newsletters or websites.**

Within the document there are gaps in the text. At these points there is a question with multiple choices. Four options are provided as possible alternatives to fill the gap; only one is correct. The three remaining distracters contain faults and are incorrect. People who already use English competently and with confidence would not make such faults and would notice them in the writing of other people or, perhaps, in an early draft of their own work.

The items of grammatical knowledge that will be tested are set out and explained below.

Consistency with standard written English

Each test presents you with some examples of English; only one example is acceptable as Standard English. You have to choose and identify that one. To be able to do that, you need to have an awareness of what kinds of error are possible, of the features of non-Standard English and of the appropriate, standard alternative.

This is the list of features of non-Standard English that the test covers:

- failure to observe sentence boundaries;
- abandoned or faulty constructions and sentence fragments;
- lack of cohesion;
- lack of agreement between subject and verb;
- should have/of, might have/of;
- inappropriate or incomplete verb forms;
- wrong or missing preposition, e.g. different from/than/to;
- noun/pronoun agreement error;
- determiner/noun agreement error;
- inappropriate or missing determiner;
- problems with comparatives and superlatives;
- problems with relative pronouns in subordinate clauses;
- inappropriate or missing adverbial forms.

Failure to observe sentence boundaries

Perhaps the commonest failing in adults' writing is this problem with deciding where a sentence ends and needs a full stop (see section on punctuation). Be very wary of sentences that go on and on. It is very easy to ignore that length and, worse still, the complexity that falls into the sentence as it develops. It is far better to write more sentences, varying in complexity, with some short, simple, one-clause sentences among them. For example:

> It was my great opportunity, from my experience with the previous class I knew how to make the most of the first group's ideas.

Should be:

> It was my great opportunity. From my experience with the previous class, I knew how to make the most of the first group's ideas.

Look at 'Comma' in the section on punctuation. Generally, unless you know you can write well, do not be too ambitious as a stylist. Your writing is more likely to be sound Standard English if you follow the advice about short sentences. If you are not sure whether it should be a comma or a full stop, put a full stop. In most cases, you will be safe.

HINT Use full stops more often.

Abandoned or faulty constructions and sentence fragments

A sentence should use consistent structures. It is very easy, especially if you write slowly, to lose track of the way you are writing, the structures you are using. The best way to avoid this problem is to reread what you write as you write and, particularly, to look out for any faults that you know you are prone to. Usually, the way that you begin the sentence is the way it should continue.

This is a faulty construction:

Concerned about the falling numbers in the city's schools so the Director of Education proposed that two primary schools should be closed and one re-opened as a junior school.

It should be either:

Concerned about the falling numbers in the city's schools, the Director of Education proposed that two primary schools should be closed and one re-opened as a junior school.

or:

The Director of Education proposed that two primary schools should be closed and one re-opened as a junior school because he was concerned about the falling numbers in the city's schools.

or:

Because he was concerned about the falling numbers in the city's schools, the Director of Education proposed that two primary schools should be closed and one re-opened as a junior school.

This is a sentence fragment:

Although there was still uncertainty about the best choice of software.

This has obviously become separated from the sentence of which it should be a part. In a sense, this is the other side of the previous problem with sentence boundaries: this time, the writer has probably put in an unnecessary full stop that cuts this fragment off from the rest. The whole sentence might have looked like this:

Although there was still uncertainty about the best choice of software, the Governors decided to go ahead with the purchase of new computers.

Here, the full sentence is given and the whole is much easier to grasp. The word 'sentence' is notoriously difficult to define but those criteria of completeness and comprehensibility are central.

An alternative to that whole sentence would be:

The Governors decided to go ahead with the purchase of new computers although there was still uncertainty about the best choice of software.

It is worth noting here, as in some other examples in this book, that there are often at least two ways to structure a sentence, often with little or no change to the words themselves. What has been altered here in the two acceptable alternatives is the sequence of the two clauses and the punctuation: if the minor (subordinate or dependent) clause comes first, separate it from the following main clause with a comma.

> **HINT**   Get into the habit, when you read a text, of seeing if some of its sentences can be restructured.

Lack of cohesion

Most of us think of grammar as the way that words are combined to make phrases, clauses and sentences. In recent decades, a lot of attention has been paid to the way that sentences are also linked together so that we know that this series of sentences is one text, not a random collection from different texts. All of us automatically use a variety of ways to make our writing (and our speech) link together as a whole, to give it cohesion.

Lack of cohesion is what happens when the writer has not made the links between sentences – or within them – as clear as they would be if they were cohesive. Cohesion deals with the various ways in which writers create these clear links. The test focuses on one of these ways, the cohesive link that depends on the appropriate use of pronouns (see the section on punctuation, and *Cohesion*, *Connective* and *Pronoun* in the Glossary).

This short passage lacks cohesion:

> A first-year **student** should receive good support from the tutors and from the student union. Nevertheless, **they** have substantial responsibility.

What is wrong here is that the noun *student* is singular but the pronoun that refers to it, *they*, is plural. This is a common error and can only be rectified by rereading as you write, checking each use of a pronoun and making sure that there is no ambiguity about which noun it refers to.

The two sentences above should read:

> First-year **students** should receive good support from the tutors and from the student union. Nevertheless, **they** have substantial responsibility.

Here, both the noun and its pronoun are plural. Sometimes the pronoun needs to be changed and sometimes, as here, it is easier to change the noun. It would be possible to revise the two problem sentences like this:

> A first-year **student** should receive good support from the tutors and from the student union but would, nevertheless, have substantial responsibility.

Here, there would be a problem in choosing a pronoun because English has only *he* or *she*, neither of which is acceptable here. One way to get round this little problem is to leave out the pronoun altogether, as the sentence above shows. That omission of a word that would normally be present is another kind of **cohesive device**: ellipsis.

Lack of agreement between subject and verb

This is another very common error. It can show itself in many ways:

- two nouns (e.g. *maths and English*) with a singular verb (e.g. *is*);
- plural determiner (e.g. *these*) with a singular verb (e.g. *was*);
- singular determiner (e.g. *this*) with a plural verb (e.g. *were*);
- singular verb (e.g. *is*) with some non-English plurals (e.g. *data*).

Here are some examples of those four basic kinds of error.

Two nouns with a singular verb:

*Underlying the good SAT results **was** the hard **work** of the pupils and a determined **staff**.*

This should be:

*Underlying the good SAT results **were** the hard **work** of the pupils and a determined **staff**.*

The subject of the verb *was* is plural: *work* and *staff*; two nouns make a plural subject. If the subject is plural, the verb should be plural: *were*.

Plural determiner with a singular verb:

***Some** teachers who had been trained in ICT **has** made excellent use of word processing.*

Some is a plural determiner – it introduces a plural noun, *teachers* – so it needs a plural verb: *have*, not *has*. That sentence should read:

***Some** teachers who had been trained in ICT **have** made excellent use of word processing.*

Singular determiner with a plural verb:

*Many of us grew up with a very prescriptive view of language without realising that **that** view of grammar **were** inadequate.*

The second use of *that* is a singular determiner so it needs a singular verb: *was*, not *were*.

That sentence should read:

*Many of us grew up with a very prescriptive view of language without realising that **that** view of grammar **was** inadequate.*

As you probably noticed, most of these determiners can also function as pronouns.

Singular verb with some non-English plurals:

> *There was some argument about the findings because the research **criteria was** in dispute.*

The word *criteria* is a plural because it comes from Greek and follows a Greek way of forming plurals. The singular form is *criterion*. Since *criteria* is plural, the verb should be *were*:

> *There was some argument about the findings because the research **criteria were** in dispute.*

An equally safe version would be:

> *There was some argument about the findings because the research **criterion was** in dispute.*

Of course, the meanings of the two sentences would be different!

English uses many words that still have their original forms of singular and plural. Some people feel that, when they are used in English, those singular and plural forms should still be used. At the moment, for instance, it seems that there is still a useful distinction in English between *criterion* and *criteria* that is worth retaining. On the other hand, some foreign loan-words are known in English in either, predominantly, a plural form (for example, *graffiti, agenda, data*) or a singular form (for example, *rhododendron*). Few of us talk of *graffito* or *rhododendra* for the simple reason that we do not know the Italian or Greek plurals (and, if we did, who – or whom – would we talk to?).

All language changes and that applies to Standard English as well as to other varieties. It is likely that words like *data* will settle down as singular forms because nobody else uses them as plural. Perhaps *data* itself will become both singular and plural, rather like *sheep*. *Criterion* and *criteria* are easier words to use confidently because both are used quite widely in British English. The point about using Standard English is to use the variety of it that is being used and understood currently.

This degree of uncertainty also applies to some other parts of this book. You will find at least as much uncertainty about these and other matters in Bill Bryson's helpful book, *Troublesome Words*.

Of all the words that still use their original, foreign plural forms, *data* and *criteria* are probably the ones most likely to be used by people in education.

Should have/of, might have/of

English makes a lot of use of modal verbs like *would, could, must, need not* and *ought to*, followed by the verb *have*. When we speak, we usually abbreviate *have* to a sound that we write as *'ve*. So we write *might have, should have*, etc. The pronunciation of *could've* is almost identical to that of *could of*, which is an error. The pronunciation of *should've, must've, would've*, etc. (the abbreviations of *should have, must have, would have*, etc.) accounts for the frequent confusions of *should of, must of, would of*, etc. It is always wrong to write *of* in these constructions. It is always right to write *have*.

*In the headteacher's view, the school might not **of** been put under Special Measures if the stable staffing the school had benefited from earlier had been maintained.*

This should read:

*In the headteacher's view, the school might not **have** been put under Special Measures if the stable staffing the school had benefited from earlier had been maintained.*

It is always worth bearing in mind that written Standard English is different from any spoken English in many ways and that it is not safe to rely too much on the sounds that are spoken as a guide to the way that the words are written. Nobody pronounces the last letter in *comb* but most of us put it in when we write the word.

Inappropriate or incomplete verb forms

One recommendation that is made repeatedly in this book is to reread what you write as you write. Even good writers can make embarrassing mistakes if they do not check what they write (this is being written by someone who consistently typed *the* as *teh* until he persuaded the Tools/Autocorrect facility to sort it out automatically). Whole words can be missed out, especially if the writer's attention is focused on another bit of the content. You need to be aware of this tendency that we all have and to pay particular attention to a fairly common error: the verb form that is either not appropriate or that is missing altogether.

Most of the class had learned use the spell check by half-term.

This should read:

*Most of the class had learned **to** use the spell check by half-term.*

One possible factor affecting this problem is that there are constructions in American English that do omit the word *to*: for example, *That afternoon, the class decided to **go explore** the neighbouring building site*. In British English, the word *to* would be used: *That afternoon, the class decided to **go to explore** the neighbouring building site*. The test is based on British English.

Sometimes, the verb itself gets left out:

Later, most of the children to show their findings to the headteacher.

This should read:

*Later, most of the children **wanted** to show their findings to the headteacher.*

It should be obvious that *wanted* is not the only verb that could fit this space but some verb, in an appropriate tense, is certainly needed.

> **HINT** This is one area where, as a writer, you can rely on the way you use language when speaking.

Wrong or missing preposition, e.g. different from/than/to

Words like *with*, *near*, *to*, *towards*, *through*, *in*, *by*, etc. are prepositions. They are usually found between two nouns (*a cat **on** a mat*), a verb and a noun (*a cat sat **on** a mat*) or some other part of speech and a noun or pronoun (*older **than**.*) Despite what was said above, there are some bits of language that change very slowly, if at all, and prepositions are among them. We still use the same prepositions that our ancestors used centuries ago. Prepositions are a *closed* word class.

The problem with them – and it is a problem; adult users of English probably have more trouble with prepositions than with any other part of speech – is that it is very easy to use an inappropriate one. This can alter what we are trying to say and cause misunderstanding.

There are some prepositions that use more than one word: complex prepositions, such as *different from*. An alternative to this is *different to*. At the moment, the complex preposition *different than* is considered to be non-Standard English. In that case, do not use it in formal writing; that is, in most writing.

The performance of this year's Y2 class was quite different than last year's.

should be either:

The performance of this year's Y2 class was quite different from last year's.

or:

The performance of this year's Y2 class was quite different to last year's.

Noun/pronoun agreement error

If you substitute pronouns for nouns in these sentences, you will notice a change in the pronouns but not in the nouns:

The man liked the woman.

becomes:

He liked her.

The woman liked the man.

becomes:

She liked him.

Two nouns have become four pronouns.

Aloysius assaulted the entire staff of the school.

becomes:

He assaulted them.

The entire staff of the school wanted to exclude Aloysius.

becomes:

They wanted to exclude him.

Man, woman, Aloysius, entire staff of the school all remained the same wherever they were in the sentences and whatever job they were doing. Nouns do not change according to position and job (although they can take a plural *s/es* and a possessive *'s* or *s'*). On the other hand, pronouns change a lot:

I	*me*	*my*	*mine*	*myself*
you	*you*	*your*	*yours*	*yourself*
she	*her*	*her*	*hers*	*herself*
he	*him*	*his*	*his*	*himself*
it	*it*	*its*	*its*	*itself*
we	*us*	*our*	*ours*	*ourselves*
they	*them*	*their*	*theirs*	*themselves*

Some years ago, the Prime Minister of the day rejected criticisms 'about Mr Lamont and I'. That is a very common error that is easy to avoid if you ask yourself what you would put if Mr Lamont were not involved. Would you write or say:

about I

or would you say:

about me

The basic rule is to ignore the use of the pronouns (whether *he and I* or *her and me* or whichever) and to ask yourself: 'Would I use *I* here or would I use *me*?' So, just as you would almost certainly write:

I have an interview in Wythenshawe next week.

You should also write:

My friend and I have interviews in Wythenshawe next week.

As you would almost certainly write:

The head showed me round the school.

You should also write:

The head showed my friend and me round the school.

To write:

The head showed my friend and I round the school.

is an unusual example of non-Standard English, unusual because it is not the English of working-class users but that spoken by middle- or aspiring middle-class users of English who believe that the *he and I* form seems more acceptable. It isn't.

Try to remember a simple sentence, such as:

I love my mother.

The word *I* comes before the verb *love* and, because it comes before the verb in this very simple sentence, it is the subject of the verb and of the sentence. If you write:

My mother loves me.

the subject is *My mother.* You do not do the loving, you *are* the loved. You are the object of the verb and of the sentence. *I* is different from *me* because it has a different meaning and does a different job.

Determiner/noun agreement error

In a radio broadcast some years ago, the then Secretary of State for Education referred to:

Those sort of programmes.

This is the error that happens when you get confused about how to link a determiner – words like *all, some, three, many, that, those, my, the, a/an* – to its noun. Such errors happen most often in brief phrases followed by a verb. This sentence-opening is accept-able English:

Determiner	noun phrase	verb …
This	*type of error*	*is …*

It is acceptable because the determiner and the verb are singular and so is the *headword* of the noun phrase, *type.* You need to know which word in the phrase is the headword, the real centre of the phrase. If the headword is singular, the verb and the determiner should also be singular. If the headword is plural, the verb and the determiner should also be plural. It is common to find sentences like this:

Although drafting and redrafting have been requirements since the 1989 National Curriculum in English, these kinds of activity is stumbling blocks for many children.

This should be:

Although drafting and redrafting have been requirements since the 1989 National Curriculum in English, these kinds of activity are stumbling blocks for many children.

This error, which is far more widespread in speech, is easy to understand but it is still not acceptable as Standard English. The writer has been trapped into using the singular verb *is* because the nearest word that *looks* like a subject – but is not – is the singular noun *activity.* In noun-phrases like:

sorts of book

kinds of poetry

types of text

the headword in every case is a plural: *sorts*, *kinds*, *types*. That plural headword is followed by a preposition and a singular noun. The next word is likely to be a verb and, in Standard English, the verb has to agree with the headword of the noun phrase; that is, if the headword is plural, the verb should be plural, too.

So should the determiner.

Inappropriate or missing determiner

The singular determiners *this*, *that* and the plural determiners *these*, *those* are also called demonstrative pronouns. We said earlier that many determiners also act as pronouns.

If you were writing about your plans for the next half-term, you might begin:

> *Mike needed to make sure that **the** key points made at **the** university Open Day were reflected in his personal statement.*

You would not – and should not – begin:

> *Mike needed to make sure that **those** key points made at **that** university Open Day were reflected in his personal statement.*

What is wrong about the second usage is that the determiners *those* and *that* refer back to something that has already been said and this is the opening so nothing has been said. *The* is wholly appropriate in this case because it introduces and establishes what you are going to write about.

Problems with comparatives and superlatives

The computer that this is being written on is new but it is not as new as the one my friend recently bought. His computer is *newer*. He says that his son, being something of an expert in these matters, has just bought a computer that is so new that nothing newer exists! That computer is – for the moment – the newest.

We are all used to making comparisons between things and people. In Standard English, this is done by using one of the two comparative forms: add *-er* to an adjective, as happened with *new/newer*, or precede it with *more*, as with *more recent*. If we want to state the ultimate in such a series, it is superlative: superlatives are expressed by adding *-est*, as with *newest*, or by preceding the adjective with *most*, as in *most recent*.

In most cases, it makes sense to write sentences that contain comparatives or superlatives but not both.

> *If children are put into groups according to whatever seating arrangements suit the activity best, the result seems to be a class that is **calmest** and **more attentive**.*

This should be:

> If children are put into groups according to whatever seating arrangements suit the activity best, the result seems to be a class that is **calmer** and **more attentive.**

It is hard to imagine a situation where it would be appropriate to write *calmer and most attentive*. To avoid this, simply reread it yourself and ask if it feels as though it makes good sense.

Since the comparison between the computers mentioned earlier obviously depended on there being another computer to compare with the first, it was necessary to bring in a third computer to see which was the newest. Superlatives are used when three or more things are being compared and comparatives when two only are being compared. Yet it is common to write or say sentences like:

> Pawel is the **tallest** twin.

This should be:

> Pawel is the **taller** twin.

There are only two twins so a comparative form of *tall* is all that is needed.

> **HINT** Alice is tall; Lucy is the taller of the *two*; Annie and Joe are the smallest of the four cousins. Compare two, it's *taller*; compare three or more, one will be *tallest*.

Problems with relative pronouns in subordinate clauses

First, we will look at **subordinate clauses**.

Suppose you write a simple sentence, with one clause, a main clause; something like this:

> I still need some information about my new class.

You can say something more, perhaps about why you need that information; something like this:

> I still need some information about my new class so that I can plan to help them.

What you have added to that main clause is another one, subordinate to it, that is called, reasonably enough, a subordinate clause. It needs the main clause to make full sense. It is a clause because it has a verb – *can plan* – and a subject – *I*.

Next, look at **relative pronouns**. These are pronouns that can introduce a subordinate clause. Most subordinate clauses are introduced by connectives such as **and, so that, because, if, unless, although**. Some, however, are introduced by a pronoun. These relative pronouns refer back to a noun in the main clause. The relative pronouns are:

> who, whom, which, that

They appear in sentences like these:

*The headteacher believed that the school needed a teacher **who** could develop ICT work.*

*After a lot of discussion, the interviewing panel agreed to appoint the candidate **whom** the headteacher preferred.*

*The Chair of the interviewing panel restated the criteria **which** they had drawn up.*

*The result of the interviews was one **that** the whole panel was happy with.*

It is also possible to leave out the relative pronoun in many cases. This sentence:

*She was the one **whom** they wanted.*

could also be written as:

*She was the one **that** they wanted.*

but also as:

She was the one they wanted.

The likely error that some fall into is to use a relative pronoun that is not appropriate. **Which** is the pronoun we use when we are dealing with inanimate things. It is appropriate in this sentence:

*Over the term, the class had read texts **which** really extended their range of interests and abilities.*

It is not appropriate in this sentence because teachers are not inanimate:

*They had chosen the teacher **which** the headteacher wanted.*

That should be either:

*They had chosen the teacher **whom** the headteacher wanted.*

or:

They had chosen the teacher the head wanted.

When do you use **who** and when do you use **whom**? Whether you should use **who** or **whom** is the same question as whether to use **he** or **him**, **she** or **her**, **I** or **me**, **we** or **us**. Suppose you are writing a very formal piece and you try the two options in this sentence:

*The panel chose the candidate **who/whom** was best.*

Ask yourself whether you would be more likely to write:

She was best.

or:

Her was best.

Unless you have a very unusual and inadequate grasp of English, you would say *She was best.* That means you would choose *who.* On the other hand, if you wanted to write this sentence:

*The headteacher asked the rest of the panel **who/whom** they liked.*

You could ask yourself whether it would make more sense to write:

They liked she.

or:

They liked her.

You would choose *her* and so you would also choose *whom.*

Although many of us hardly ever use *whom*, especially when speaking, the test is based on formal writing and does expect it to be used.

Inappropriate or missing adverbial forms

Sometimes, we can confuse the use of an adjective and an adverb. We know that we can write:

Mushraf was a fast runner.

where *fast* is an adjective, rather like *quick*. However, we can also write:

Mushraf ran fast.

where *fast* is an adverb, just like *quickly.* We know that many adverbs do not end in *-ly*. This very reliable bit of knowledge might tempt some of us to write sentences like this, where an adjective is used instead of an adverb:

On the whole, student options were intelligent chosen.

This should be:

On the whole, student options were intelligently chosen.

This is not the sort of error that native users of a language tend to make but it is the sort that can easily creep into a written text. That is why we repeatedly advise you to read and reread as you write. Get a feel for the sense and the flow of what you write and for the tone of voice you are using as a writer.

Sense, clarity and freedom from ambiguity

Some fiction and much poetry deliberately make very profitable use of the ambiguities and optional meanings that can be made from language. Most writing, however, has to make clarity a priority. Make your writing as easy to read as possible; change anything that is ambiguous; check it all the time to make sure that it makes sense.

You will be tested on your ability to spot when a piece of writing is clear and when it is not. This means that you need to have a good idea of the place that grammar can play in helping a text to be clear. The test will show you examples of writing and ask you to identify which of several options would make the piece clear.

These are some of the factors that make writing unclear:

Lack of coherence

Some texts are easier to read than others. If it is easy to understand, it must be coherent: it has *coherence*; the bits hold together to make a whole. Writers use a variety of ways to make this happen; for example, that pronoun *this* refers back to the idea of coherence in the previous sentence. Pronouns are crucial in making links *between* sentences in a continuous text.

Writers use other devices to make clauses hold together *within* a sentence. For example, they use *connectives* so that one clause can be linked in meaning to another; in this sentence, *so that* is a connective, linking the main clause *they use connectives* to its subordinate clause.

That use of grammatical devices to create that coherence is called *cohesion*. Those devices are called *cohesive devices*. There are several others that are not discussed here.

In the test, you will be asked to identify when a text lacks coherence because there are problems with:

- tense;
- unrelated participles; or
- an ambiguous use of pronouns.

These are all explained below.

Wrong tense or tense inconsistency

Tense is the aspect of a verb that deals with time. It is possible to use more than one tense in one sentence, as in this:

> My father **was** a sheet-metal worker, I **am** a teacher and my daughter **is going to be** a teacher.

The first verb, *was*, is a form of the past tense; the second, *am*, is a form of the present; the third, *is going to be*, is a form of the future tense.

Other forms of the past include *has been, used to be*. Other forms of the present include *am being* (with verbs other than **be**, the present can also use *do*, as in *do like, do care*, etc.). Other forms of the future include *will be*.

There is no problem with the use of different tenses in that simple sentence. That is because the meaning of the sentence really is about different times so it is right to use different tenses. The key to all this is to keep a close eye on what you mean to write, what tense fits what you are trying to say. Keep rereading and checking! If you do, you are less likely to use tenses inconsistently, the commonest failing with this aspect of written grammar.

> **HINT**   Over time, you will strengthen your grasp of tense if you read fairly quickly. Slow readers – and writers – easily lose track of what happens when.

*Shahida began his book at half-term and **finishes** it last week.*

should be:

*Shahida began his book at half-term and **finished** it last week.*

Began and *finished* are both verbs in the past tense. That fits the meaning of the sentence and is therefore consistent. It would also be consistent if the truth was this:

Shahida began his book at half-term and will finish it next week.

There, *began* is in the past tense and *will finish* is in the future tense but the sentence is grammatically consistent because it fits the meaning.

A sentence such as:

*The staff will have written their reports by Friday and so **met** the deadline.*

should be:

*The staff will have written their reports by Friday and so **will meet** the deadline.*

In the first sentence, the staff have not yet completed the reports so it is not true to say they have already met a deadline. That does not make sense and so is inconsistent.

Unrelated participles

What are participles and in what ways might they be unrelated? In a sentence such as:

The school had closed for Easter.

the word *closed* follows a subject, the noun *school*, and immediately follows a form of the verb *to have*. A word that could do that is a **participle**, a part of the verb which expresses tense (in this case, a form of the past tense). Past participles often end in *-ed* but may end in *-en* (*written*), *-n* (*shown*), *-d* (*read*) or *-t* (*thought*).

In a sentence such as:

The school is closing for Easter.

the word *closing* follows a subject, the noun *school*, and immediately follows a form of the verb *to be*. Therefore, *closing* is also a participle and it expresses a form of the present tense.

A participle never has a subject, such as the pronouns *I, you, she, he, it, we, they*, immediately before it; the verb *to be* or *to have* has to come between them, as in the examples above.

Participles can be found in some clauses of this type:

Collaborating with someone who has more competence, a learner can be helped to construct new meanings.

In that sentence, the question of who does the *collaborating* is answered by the subject of the next clause: *the learner.* That is an example of a *related participle*; the participle is unambiguously related to a subject. However, the participle is not related to the subject in a sentence like this:

Collaborating with someone who has more competence, the teacher can help the learner to construct new meanings.

Here, the subject of that second clause is the teacher but the person who collaborates with someone who has more competence is the learner. The participle, *collaborating*, is *unrelated* to the subject, *the teacher.*

Unrelated participles are unacceptable because they are confusing and may be ambiguous. They should be avoided.

The sentence:

Being well-managed, the head of Armitage School could afford to employ a 0.5 teaching assistant after Christmas.

is unacceptable because it is the school that is well-managed, not the head. The sentence:

Providing far more than the national average of free dinners, Seddon Junior School might be expected to have considerable problems.

is acceptable because there is no doubt that it is the school that provides many free dinners.

Attachment ambiguities

Always keep an eye on the meaning of what you write or read. This book stresses that again and again but it is clear from what many people write that this advice is easily overlooked.

For example, if you wrote:

> *The headteacher told me about the exclusion appeal.*

you could add to that sentence a phrase about when the appeal was to be held. Where would that phrase appear? If you wrote:

> ***On Monday,*** *the headteacher told me about the exclusion appeal.*

that states unambiguously that Monday was the day that you were told. If you wrote:

> *The headteacher told me about the exclusion appeal **on Monday.***

the change of position now *implies* that the appeal will take place on Monday. The problem is that it still allows the reader to *infer* that Monday was when you heard about the appeal. Does the phrase **on Monday** refer to the verb *told* or to the noun *appeal*? One sentence has two possible meanings although one – the timing of the appeal – is the more likely because *appeal* and *on Monday* appear close to each other.

It is easy to avoid this ambiguity by turning that added two-word phrase into a clause, as in:

> *The headteacher told me about the exclusion appeal **that would take place on Monday.***

Vague or ambiguous pronoun reference

This kind of ambiguity is very common. In children's writing, it is very common indeed. One of the best activities that teachers can demonstrate, model and encourage is how to redraft a piece of writing by checking that there is no ambiguity about which nouns the pronouns refer to. Unless children (and other writers!) write quickly enough to be able to keep in mind what they are writing as they write, and unless they check what they write, it is very likely that they will use pronouns such as *he, she, it, they* (and the other forms of the pronoun, such as *him, her, them*, etc.) in ways that do not refer clearly to their nouns.

> *All the new computers and most of the stationery materials have been stored in the old stock cupboards. Nothing more can be done with **them** until the electrician arrives.*

should be:

> *All the new computers and most of the stationery materials have been stored in the old stock cupboards. Nothing more can be done with the computers until the electrician arrives.*

Unless the computers are specified – and that means using the noun, not the pronoun – it seems as if the electrician has to do something with the stationery as well. This would be, at least, confusing.

Clarity matters and, therefore, so does explicitness: that means using nouns instead of pronouns if it would be confusing to do otherwise.

> *Liam and Aloysius took Ryan and Nathan to see if **their** food was ready.*

should be:

Liam and Aloysius took Ryan and Nathan to see if all their food was ready.

or:

Liam and Aloysius took Ryan and Nathan to see if Liam's and Aloysius' food was ready.

or:

Liam and Aloysius took Ryan and Nathan to see if Ryan's and Nathan's food was ready.

Which you use depends on your meaning. Some of these seem clumsy but even clumsiness is better than confusion. This particular confusion is very common in children's writing.

Confusion of words, e.g. imply/infer

All varieties of all languages change all the time. That is the single most obvious fact about language. Using Standard English does not mean using the language of a century or two ago if it is very different from usage today. On the other hand, many older usages are still widespread among literate users of English so you are advised still to follow that variety of Standard English.

One usage that seems to be common can cause real problems with understanding. English has many words that look and sound rather alike and so are sometimes used interchangeably but their meanings are quite different. If you say to a fairly educated person that you are *disinterested* about the children you teach, you should get some approval because it means that you are impartial, not that you are uninterested. So:

Just because I said I didn't mind teaching either Y3 or Y4, the headteacher thinks I'm **disinterested***.*

should be:

Just because I said I didn't mind teaching either Y3 or Y4, the head thinks I'm **uninterested***.*

If you have no great preference, you really are *disinterested*!

The words *infer* and *imply* are more often misused than not. *Infer* is used far more often than *imply* and often it is used wrongly.

He **inferred** *that I'm not bothered who I teach.*

should be:

He **implied** *that I'm not bothered who [to be formal, whom] I teach.*

The odd thing about this particular confusion is that the words are almost opposite. If you imply something to a friend, your friend should infer the same message from you. *Infer* means *conclude*, as in:

*From the way he was talking about falling numbers, I **inferred** that there could be a redundancy soon.*

Imply means to *suggest something without directly saying so*, as in:

*I know she didn't say definitely but she **implied** that she might have a job for me next term.*

Here are some other words that are often confused:

Except in uncommon usages such as: *The staff room had been burgled when someone **effected** an entry from the playground side,* the word effect is used as a noun:

*Unexpectedly, the music had a calming **effect** on a usually unruly class.*

Affect is almost always a verb, as in:

*Yes, the music definitely **affected** them strongly.*

Rebut, refute and **deny** are sometimes used as though they were interchangeable. Their meanings are related but distinct:

*When I implied that the deputy had forgotten about the Theatre in Education visit, she **refuted** what I had said by showing me the letter she had written to book the visit.*

Here, the deputy head proved that the implied accusation was wrong by providing evidence; she *refuted* it.

*She was angry and **rebutted** the accusation, calling me a nasty-minded trouble-maker who should think about a suitable job, such as pig-farming.*

The deputy is more emotional and does not bother with the evidence.

*All she needed to do was to **deny** it.*

The accuser now wishes that the deputy had restricted herself to a mere denial, without proving the point and without the anger. *Deny* can be an angry verb and it can involve proof but something else has to be added to make those points: *denied angrily, denied the accusation and showed the proof.*

Here are some other words that may get confused:

Discrete means separate, individually distinct, discontinuous (OED) not continuous; **discreet** means able to avoid embarrassing others – or yourself:

*Some of his sentences were a list of **discrete** words, unconnected by any grammatical device.*

but:

*There was so much rumour in the air that we all appreciated having such a **discreet** colleague.*

Accept means to receive something, particularly without fuss; *except* means that some-body or something is not part of a general situation:

   The head **accepted** my apology and carried on conducting the assembly himself.

but:

   After the staff meeting, the head dismissed everybody **except** me.

Contemptuous means that the subject feels contempt for somebody or something; *con-temptible* is what that somebody or something is:

   My tutor was quite **contemptuous** of my efforts.

but:

   Privately, even I had to agree that they really were **contemptible**.

Militate means to have an influence against some evidence; *mitigate* means to reduce an effect, to soften or to appease:

   The latest SAT results **militate** against the last inspection report.

but:

   The clarity and liveliness of Jeannie's story **mitigated** her general performance in school.

Continuous means that something is without a break; *continual* means that something happens regularly:

   On their way to the swimming baths, the class walked in a **continuous** line.

but:

   There is a **continual** outburst of delight every Friday.

Different means that *this* is not like *that*; *differing* means that opinions or evidence clash:

   This year's Y6 class is quite **different** from last year's.

but:

   The staff sat in silence as the **differing** views of the headteacher and her deputy thickened the air of the tiny staff room.

Allusion means a rather indirect reference to something that you probably know about; *illusion* means an idea that does not fit reality:

*Without mentioning any names or any events, the head made an **allusion** to the incident at the outdoor pursuits centre that lost the school its best speller.*

but:

*The miscalculated test results caused us to live in a happy **illusion** until the SATs brought in reality.*

Stationary means without movement; **stationery** means paper, pens, etc.:

*Luckily, the class knew they had to be quite **stationary** before crossing a busy road.*

but:

*We were distraught by the lack of paper until the **stationery** supplies arrived.*

It helps to use a dictionary often, for spellings, for meanings – especially shades of meaning – and simply to get into the habit of using a valuable source of information. Other books, such as Bill Bryson's *Troublesome Words*, may also help.

Professional suitability and style

All native users of a language learn, from their earliest experiences of it, to match their style to their audience, to their own purpose in speaking or writing and to the topic being discussed. This test is about your ability to tell the difference between appropriate and inappropriate style. In particular, try to avoid these stylistic usages:

Non-parallelism in lists

When you write a list, look at the words you use to introduce the list. Each item in the list should follow grammatically from that introduction:

In future planning, I should remember to:

a. *to plan who should be in each group;*
b. *friendship groups.*

should be:

In future planning, I should remember to:

a. *plan who should be in each group;*
b. *consider friendship groups.*

No native user of English would say or write:

In future planning, I should remember to to plan who should be in each group.

or:

In future planning, I should remember to friendship groups.

Inconsistent register and tone

We can make a mistake with the tone of what we write. This is usually because we use a tone that is too formal or one that is too informal. Most writing is formal so a formal style is more appropriate in most cases.

An inconsistent style can show itself in the use of colloquialisms:

*It was reported last night that the Secretary of State was **doing her nut** over the slow progress of her latest initiative for small rural schools.*

The opening phrase, *'It was reported'*, implies that the speaker was a newsreader and the intended audience the general public. *'Doing her nut'* is inappropriate in a news report. The tone and style should be appropriate to the audience.

This would be more consistent in tone if it was written like this:

*It was reported last night that the Secretary of State was **concerned** over the slow progress of her latest initiative for small rural schools.*

An inconsistency of tone can also be created by mixing the use of active and passive constructions in the same sentence:

*Some of the children **opened** [active] the letters for home, **read** [active] them and **were torn up** [passive].*

should be either:

*Some of the children **opened** [active] the letters for home, **read** [active] them and **tore them up** [active].*

or:

*Some of the letters for home **were opened** [passive] by the children, **read** [passive] and **torn up** [passive].*

In this last example, the auxiliary verb *were* has been left out from *were read* and *were torn up*. That is another case of *ellipsis*, what Dan Slobin calls *optional deletion*.

Finally, an inconsistent tone can also be created by mixing the use of the informal *you* and the more formal *one* in the same sentence. *You* is almost universal in speech, in sentences such as:

You never can tell.

You is also appropriate in writing, especially informal writing; it is also appropriate in fairly formal writing. What is inappropriate is to mix the two styles:

*Since **you** played such an active role in last year's Easter Fair, **one** should take up the challenge again this year.*

should be:

> Since **you** played such an active role in last year's Easter Fair, **you** should take up the challenge again this year.

On the other hand:

> Although **you** always found that the middle term used to be the most productive, **one** finds the level of production more evenly spread over the year now.

should be:

> Although **one** always found that the middle term used to be the most productive, **one** finds the level of production more evenly spread over the year now.

or:

> Although **I** always found that the middle term used to be the most productive, **I** find the level of production more evenly spread over the year now.

Both *one* and *you* can mean *people in general* or *people like us* or *me*. *You* can sometimes be confusing if it both carries that very general meaning and also means the other person. In other words, *you* is usually a second person pronoun, coming between *I* and *she/he/it*, and it can be confusing if it is used as a third person pronoun like *one*.

Be consistent.

Shift in person within sentences or across sentences

This is related to the last point above. Like that, it is related to what happens when formal and informal styles or register get mixed. It is also related to *cohesion* and the use of pronouns. If you mean the same people, do not confuse things by referring to them as *you* when you really mean *they*:

> Too many **people** are leaving doors open when **you** shouldn't.

should be:

> Too many **people** are leaving doors open when **they** shouldn't.

or:

> Too many **of you** are leaving doors open when **you** shouldn't.

> **One** hopes that the new community room will be ready before next term begins so that **we** can make full use of it.

should be:

> **We** hope that the new community room will be ready before next term begins so that **we** can make full use of it.

Many problems with writing can be reduced greatly if you get into and keep the habit of reading what you write as you write it, rereading chunks and checking it at the end. Keep an eye on what you mean to say.

Excessive length and rambling sentences

This issue is related to earlier ones about abandoned constructions and failures to observe sentence boundaries. The key point is to see if very long sentences can be rewritten as more than one sentence. Long sentences are more than acceptable but only if the writer can control them:

Charlie is obviously a child that although has developed a high level of phonic understanding and is capable of breaking down unknown words is still with my regards to the definition of a reader not successful.

should be:

Charlie obviously has a high level of phonic understanding. He is able to break down unknown words. However, he is still not a successful reader in my view.

The uncorrected sentence above is a genuine product of a trainee teacher. So is the following sentence:

With certain aspects of literacy I agree with Yetta Goodman (1980) whose research indicated that literacy is a naturally occurring and developing process in 'our literate society', however, this development is minimal in comparison with the expected requirements, for example children may naturally occur certain literacy skills.

should be:

Concerning certain aspects of literacy, I agree with Yetta Goodman (1980) whose research indicated that literacy is a naturally occurring and developing process in our literate society. This development is minimal in comparison with the expected requirements. For example, children may naturally acquire certain literacy skills.

You might have noticed that the uncorrected version has other problems, unconnected with sentence length or boundary. Problems rarely come singly.

Redundancy/tautology

If an expression means what you want to say, there is no need to add to it. It would make no sense to refer to the *STA Agency* because the acronym means *Standards and Testing Agency*.

*The headteacher reported that the governing body had **definitely** excluded Aloysius.*

should be:

The headteacher reported that the governing body had excluded Aloysius.

Exclusion is itself a word with no limits so there is no point in saying that it is *definite*.

Some kinds of apparent redundancy are more problematic. One change in Standard English over recent decades is that the verb *check* has almost been replaced by *check out*. They mean the same but it could be argued that the apparently redundant *out* is now part of a developing Standard English.

Inappropriate conjunctions (also known as connectives)

Look at what was said above about relative pronouns and relative clauses in 'Problems with relative pronouns in subordinate clauses'. Clauses that begin with *who, whom, which, that* are in a different category from those that begin with one of the long list of connectives such as *if, because, unless, so that, in case, although*, etc. All these words can begin a subordinate clause but the relationship with the main clause is different.

> *The trouble with Roy is **because** he will not buckle down to hard work.*

should be:

> *The trouble with Roy is **that** he will not buckle down to hard work.*

or:

> *There is trouble with Roy **because** he will not buckle down to hard work.*

Some problems occur because the main clause has been completed and there seems to be a break in the writer's thinking before continuing with the subordinate clause:

> *Roy's improvement has been **so** dramatic **so that** he could be quite near the top this year.*

should be:

> *Roy's improvement has been dramatic **so** he could be quite near the top this year.*

or:

> *Roy's improvement has been **so** dramatic **that** he could be quite near the top this year.*

Some conjunctions occur not only between clauses but also between phrases and even between single words. The problem is that sometimes these necessary words get left out:

> *The headteacher received a long silence at the staff meeting when he announced his intention to sing dance at the interval during the Christmas play.*

should be:

> *The headteacher received a long silence at the staff meeting when he announced his intention to sing **and** dance at the interval during the Christmas play.*

Remember that you will not be tested on all the items in this section nor is this list a syllabus. A glance at the sheer bulk of any grammar text should remind you that this is not exhaustive.

If you get stuck at any point, reread what you have done, ask if it makes clear sense and see if it is as consistent with the rest of the sentence, paragraph or text as you can make it.

Questions

The actual test is computerised. You will be shown part of a sentence and then presented with a range of optional clauses or phrases that might complete the sentence. Decide which would be the best option to complete the sentence grammatically and drag it into the space provided. The test in this book involves you in precisely the same kind of thinking as the computerised test.

The grammar section of the test asks you to complete some sentences. That tests your ability to detect when something is wrong. You will see the first part of a sentence and then four optional ways to complete it. Three of these options are wrong or unsatisfactory in some way. Your task is to choose the best way to complete the sentence.

There are three tests of grammar:

- of your ability to detect unrelated participles;
- of your ability to detect the wrong tense or tense inconsistency;
- of your ability to detect any lack of agreement between subject and verb.

Unrelated participles

In the following tests, underline the one sentence that seems to you to be **appropriate in its use of a related participle rather than an unrelated one.**

TEST A

1. Realising the role that speech plays in helping children to solve practical tasks, it follows that children should be given tasks that require talk.

2. Realising the role that speech plays in helping children to solve practical tasks, Vygotsky placed language at the centre of all learning.

3. Realising the role that speech plays in helping children to solve practical tasks, language was seen by Vygotsky as central to learning.

4. Realising the role that speech plays in helping children to solve practical tasks, children's unassisted work is stressed by many teachers.

(Continued)

(Continued)

TEST B

1. Persuaded by her staff that afternoon playtimes were increasingly disruptive, the head decided to have no playtimes in the afternoon but to end school ten minutes early.

2. Persuaded by her staff that afternoon playtimes were increasingly disruptive, afternoon play was abandoned by the head and replaced with an earlier hometime.

3. Persuaded by her staff that afternoon playtimes were increasingly disruptive, the school exchanged its afternoon play for a shorter afternoon session.

4. Persuaded by her staff that afternoon playtimes were increasingly disruptive, the children had no play but could leave school ten minutes earlier.

TEST C

1. The curriculum, according to Peters, is not wholly an end in itself, conceding that even history can be viewed in an instrumental way.

2. Peters believes that the curriculum is not wholly an end in itself, conceding that even history can be viewed in an instrumental way.

3. Conceding that even history can be viewed in an instrumental way, the view that the curriculum is an end in itself is not fully supported by Peters.

4. Conceding that even history can be viewed in an instrumental way, Peters' view of the curriculum is not wholly in favour of education as an end in itself.

TEST D

1. Thought to be the easiest class in the school to teach, the head was surprised by the mayhem they caused during silent reading.

2. Thought to be the easiest class in the school to teach, it was surprising to the head that they could cause so much mayhem during silent reading.

3. Thought to be the easiest class in the school to teach, the mayhem they caused during silent reading was a surprise for the head.

4. Thought to be the easiest class in the school to teach, the children caused mayhem during silent reading.

Wrong tense or tense inconsistency

In the following tests, underline the one sentence that seems to you to be **appropriate in its use of the right and most consistent tense.**

TEST A

1. Although I wish now that I had worked harder, my A level results were very pleasing and it has meant being able to be more ambitious in the applications I made.

2. Although I wish now that I had worked harder, my A level results were very pleasing and it has meant that I have been able to be more ambitious in the applications I made.

3. Although I wish now that I had worked harder, my A level results were very pleasing and it has meant that I was able to be more ambitious in the applications I made.

4. Although I wish now that I had worked harder, my A level results were very pleasing and it has meant that I am able to be more ambitious in the applications I made.

TEST B

1. I don't consider myself a very gifted person, although I did well enough, but my headteacher father believes I'll make a good teacher and that, although I have always been a little naïve, life was good.

2. I don't consider myself a very gifted person, although I did well enough, but my headteacher father believes I'll make a good teacher and that, although I have always been a little naïve, life being good.

3. I don't consider myself a very gifted person, although I did well enough, but my headteacher father believes I'll make a good teacher and that, although I have always been a little naïve, life is good.

4. I don't consider myself a very gifted person, although I did well enough, but my headteacher father believes I'll make a good teacher and that, although I have always been a little naïve, life will be good.

TEST C

1. Whatever I do, my mind fills with thoughts of what could happen if I chose a course where I can't fit in, the other students don't respond, the staff are cold and unhelpful and my tutor is bad-tempered.

2. Whatever I do, my mind fills with thoughts of what could happen if I chose a course where I can't fit in, the other students don't respond, the staff are cold and unhelpful and my tutor was bad-tempered.

3. Whatever I do, my mind fills with thoughts of what could happen if I chose a course where I can't fit in, the other students don't respond, the staff are cold and unhelpful and my tutor has been bad-tempered.

(Continued)

(Continued)

4. Whatever I do, my mind fills with thoughts of what could happen if I chose a course where I can't fit in, the other students don't respond, the staff are cold and unhelpful and my tutor being bad-tempered.

TEST D

1. Perhaps the best action for me to take is to talk with friends, at least once I have examined what different areas offer, compared facilities, accommodation and opportunities and growing a little more sure of myself.

2. Perhaps the best action for me to take is to talk with friends, at least once I have examined what different areas offer, compared facilities, accommodation and opportunities and grow a little more sure of myself.

3. Perhaps the best action for me to take is to talk with friends, at least once I have examined what different areas offer, compared facilities, accommodation and opportunities and grew a little more sure of myself.

4. Perhaps the best action for me to take is to talk with friends, at least once I have examined what different areas offer, compared facilities, accommodation and opportunities and grown a little more sure of myself.

Lack of agreement between subject and verb

In the following tests, underline the one sentence that seems to you to be **appropriate in its agreement between subject and verb**.

TEST A

1. The trouble with both the way I talk and the way I write are that for much of the time I cannot trust myself to remember what I started with.

2. The trouble with both the way I talk and the way I write were that for much of the time I cannot trust myself to remember what I started with.

3. The trouble with both the way I talk and the way I write was that for much of the time I cannot trust myself to remember what I started with.

4. The trouble with both the way I talk and the way I write is that for much of the time I cannot trust myself to remember what I started with.

TEST B

1. A friend told me that the likeliest cause of this problem is that the unrelentingly abusive attitudes shown by my first English teacher is quite traumatic for me.

2. A friend told me that the likeliest cause of this problem is that the unrelentingly abusive attitudes shown by my first English teacher were quite traumatic for me.

3. A friend told me that the likeliest cause of this problem is that the unrelentingly abusive attitudes shown by my first English teacher was quite traumatic for me.

4. A friend told me that the likeliest cause of this problem is that the unrelentingly abusive attitudes shown by my first English teacher being quite traumatic for me.

TEST C

1. I wish it were that simple. In fact, are it that teacher, the one who helped me somehow to qualify for university, the sicknesses I had as a child or my supportive but rather stern parents?

2. I wish it were that simple. In fact, were it that teacher, the one who helped me somehow to qualify for university, the sicknesses I had as a child or my supportive but rather stern parents?

3. I wish it were that simple. In fact, was it that teacher, the one who helped me somehow to qualify for university, the sicknesses I had as a child or my supportive but rather stern parents?

4. I wish it were that simple. In fact, is it that teacher, the one who helped me somehow to qualify for university, the sicknesses I had as a child or my supportive but rather stern parents?

TEST D

1. As I look ahead, I know that the future, whether I am lucky or not or leave teaching or stay with it, and whatever anyone else does or says, was mine to make.

2. As I look ahead, I know that the future, whether I am lucky or not or leave teaching or stay with it, and whatever anyone else does or says, has been mine to make.

3. As I look ahead, I know that the future, whether I am lucky or not or leave teaching or stay with it, and whatever anyone else does or says, will be mine to make.

4. As I look ahead, I know that the future, whether I am lucky or not or leave teaching or stay with it, and whatever anyone else does or says, will have been mine to make.

4 | Comprehension

Introduction

8–12 marks are available for comprehension.

Most of the test is about writing. This section is about reading.

Teachers now have to read a great deal of written material about their professional lives and work. This material can be government documents (for example, on the law concerning exclusion from school), the educational press and very frequent information about the local educational scene. Because every teacher now has to do so much professionally demanding reading, there is a greater stress than there was previously on their being able to:

- identify the key points in a text;
- 'read between the lines' in order to make inferences and deductions;
- differentiate between fact and fiction in a written text;
- understand which points are more significant than others and how this relative importance affects a text;
- comprehend a text well enough to be able to re-present the meaning in a different way from the original;
- retrieve factual information and/or specific ideas from a text;
- judge whether specific comments made about a text are actually supported, implied, implicitly or explicitly contradicted, or simply not present in that text;
- summarise information from a section, or about a topic, in a text;
- identify or adapt suitable information from a text for a specific audience.

The test will expect you to be sufficiently proficient in these skills in order to complete the following tasks:

- attribute statements to categories;
- complete a bulleted list;
- sequence information;
- present main points;
- match texts to summaries;
- identify the meanings of words and phrases;
- evaluate statements about the text;
- select headings and subheadings;
- identify possible readership or audience for a text.

These are the nine possible comprehension question types.

The test you take will test only a selection of these aspects of literacy.

The comprehension test presents candidates with a short text and a series of questions on it. Read the whole text first. Good reading means paying almost simultaneous attention to the word or phrase you are concentrating on at the time and also to as much of the whole text as you have read and can keep in mind. To do this test well, you will need to focus on what is significant in the whole text so that you are able to select those bits and ignore the rest. Some questions ask you to see how this bit of the text relates to that bit, to notice how parts of the text are organised, to sequence ideas and to check what some phrases or wo. !s mean in the context. None of this is extraordinary and an attentive and reasonably experienced reader should not have difficulties.

Questions

There are nine possible comprehension question types; each Literacy Skills Test will test a selection of these. However, for the sake of this exercise, tasks have been set using all nine comprehension question types.

Read this extract from an Ofsted document and complete the following tasks.

Ofsted to revise the framework for initial teacher education (ITE)

Ofsted is proposing to raise expectations of providers of teacher training to help ensure that more trainees are better prepared with the practical skills that teachers need most, such as the ability to manage behaviour and teach reading effectively.

Feedback on the current inspection arrangements has been positive but also suggests the need to continue to raise expectations. This means drawing up clearer, more challenging criteria with fewer, more streamlined judgements and one overarching judgement for overall effectiveness. Ofsted is also seeking views on reducing the eight-week notice period for an inspection to three weeks.

Her Majesty's Chief Inspector (HMCI) of Education said, 'The quality of teaching is an essential element in any school so the selection and training of the next generation of teachers is crucial. We hope that changes to the way we inspect initial teacher education will enable inspectors to focus even more on the things that are important: teaching pupils to read, behaviour management and trainees' ability to teach a range of learners, including those with special educational needs and/or disabilities.

'Inspection helps to raise standards and ensure the best training is provided. We want more trainees to become good or outstanding teachers and gain employment in schools. This is why, in the new arrangements, we want to focus inspection afresh on observing current and former trainees in the classroom. I'd like to encourage anyone with an interest in initial teacher education, in particular those who provide training, are currently in training, or thinking of joining a teacher training programme, to tell us their views.'

(Continued)

(Continued)

Building on the strengths of the current arrangements, it is proposed that inspection will look more closely at the selection of trainees and the quality of partnerships ITE providers have with settings, schools and colleges. It will focus even more on the quality of training and trainees' subject knowledge and their understanding and competence in developing pupils' literacy skills, including using systematic phonics to teach reading. Ofsted is also considering incorporating a thematic element into inspections, on a rolling programme, in order to gain more evidence on the effectiveness of training to teach specific subjects and aspects such as managing behaviour.

The proposals include a more proportionate approach to inspection that is informed by a robust risk assessment process so inspections can be targeted where improvement is needed most. Partnerships previously judged to be satisfactory will be inspected at an early stage in the new cycle and those that continue to be satisfactory will be subject to a monitoring inspection, which will take place 12–18 months after the inspection. Finally, a full inspection is likely to take place within three years of the previous inspection.

Ofsted proposes that initial teacher education inspections will also:

- **retain the focus on trainees' outcomes at the heart of the inspection**
- **be underpinned by clear and more challenging criteria for judging partnerships to be outstanding or good**
- **take account of the views of users, trainees and former trainees, including newly qualified and recently qualified teachers**
- **use an on-line questionnaire to gather the views of trainees**
- **integrate judgements on equality and diversity throughout the report, including reporting on the performance of different groups of trainees**
- **introduce a focused monitoring inspection; for example, to look at the provision of phonics training where newly qualified teacher feedback raises concerns**
- **continue to involve leaders, managers, tutors, mentors, trainees and former trainees in discussions during an inspection**
- **continue to take account of a partnership's self-evaluation, and**
- **continue to drive improvement in the sector by providing an external evaluation of strengths and weaknesses.**

The proposals take into account feedback from providers, inspectors and other stakeholders with an interest in ITE.

Attributing statements to categories

Read the statements below and decide which refer to:

ITEP   Initial Teacher Education Providers

TT   Trainee Teachers

O   Ofsted

HMCI   Her Majesty's Chief Inspector

Put the correct code in the box to the left of each statement.

(In the computerised test, you will be asked to drag the code to the box.)

〔MUCI〕	They are going to require more from teacher training courses.
〔I.TE〕	They regard the training of the next cohort of teachers as very significant.
〔 O 〕	They are going to be expected to know how to develop literacy skills.
〔 TT 〕	They are going to have to look more closely at placements.

Completing a bulleted list

Look at the phrases below. Put a tick next to the three that most accurately complete the stem. The final one has been done for you.

(In the computerised test you will be asked to drag a number of phrases one at a time to the bulleted list.)

It is anticipated that all future ITE inspections will:

-
-
-
- **continue to take account of a partnership's self-evaluation.**

☑ target inspections only where improvement is most needed

☐ focus entirely on specific themes such as behaviour management

☑ be strengthened by tougher criteria for judging outstanding or good trainees

☐ be preceded by a notice period of only three weeks

☑ improve ITE by providing an external evaluation of strengths and weaknesses

☐ gauge the diversity of partnerships ITE providers have established

☐ be reinforced by a more demanding measure of outstanding or good partnerships

☑ take account of the views of newly or recently qualified teachers

Sequencing information

From the seven statements below select the three that most accurately reflect the order of the steps to be taken in the new cycle of inspection of the partnerships ITE providers have with their settings, schools and colleges.

Write FIRST, SECOND OR THIRD in the box to the left of your choice of statement.

(In the computerised test you will be asked to click on the labels FIRST, SECOND or THIRD, one at a time, and drag them to the boxes beside your chosen answer.)

(Continued)

(Continued)

1	All partnerships will undergo an initial risk assessment.
✗	Partnerships previously judged to be satisfactory will be inspected.
2	Those showing most need for improvement will be inspected first.
	All partnerships will be inspected within three years of this revision.
	Those that continue to be satisfactory will be inspected within 12 to 18 months.
3	Partnerships will have a full inspection within three years of a previous inspection.
	Partnership's chances of being inspected will be proportionate to their quality.

Presenting main points

From the list below, select the four points that most accurately describe Ofsted's main objectives in revising the inspection framework for ITE. Tick the box to the left of the point to indicate your four choices.

(In the computerised test you will be asked to click on your four choices, one at a time, and drag them to four empty bullet points in the adjacent box.)

☐	Gauge the effectiveness of the teaching of phonics by newly qualified teachers.
✓	Look more closely at how trainees are evaluated and selected for ITE.
☒	Scrutinise the inspection criteria used to assess teachers in schools.
☐	Encourage teachers working in schools to tell them their views on ITE.
✓	Upgrade the quality of training given by ITE providers.
☐	Ensure practical teaching skills are top of the agenda for trainees.
☑	Introduce a thematic approach into the inspection of behaviour management.
☐	Introduce one comprehensive criterion for the general effectiveness of ITE provision.
☐	Reduce the notice period given prior to inspection of ITE provision.

Matching texts to summaries

Reread paragraphs 1, 3 and 5. From the list of statements below, select the one that most accurately summarises the content of these three paragraphs. Tick the box next to your choice.

(In the computerised test you will be asked to drag a tick symbol to the box beside your choice.)

☐ It is vital to build on the strengths of the current arrangements and raise the expectations of the next generation of trainee teachers.

☐ It is time for a complete overhaul of the inspection process for ITE so that schools can focus even more on the things that are important.

☑ The most important attributes of the trainee teacher emerging from ITE are the abilities to control and manage behaviour and to teach literacy effectively.

☐ Teaching can be improved by raising expectations, introducing a more rigorous selection of trainees and improving the quality of settings, schools and colleges.

Identifying the meanings of words and phrases

Select the most suitable alternative for the phrase as it appears in the context of the passage. Tick the box next to your choice.

(*In the computerised test you will be asked to drag a tick symbol to the box beside your choice.*)

'**... raise expectations of providers of teacher training**' (paragraph 1) is closest in meaning to:

☐ investigate the endeavours of providers of teacher training

☑ lift the requirements of providers of teacher training

☐ boost the hopes of providers of teacher training

☐ increase the demands on providers of teacher training

'**... a more proportionate approach to**' (paragraph 6) is closest in meaning to:

☐ a more commensurate method of

☐ a more detached pathway to

☑ a more competitive move towards

☐ a more rigorous course of

Evaluating statements about the text

Read each of the statements below about the Ofsted revision of the framework for initial teacher education and decide which of them:

is supported by the text	**S**
is implied to be the case, or implicitly supported, by the text	**I**
states something for which there is no evidence or support in the text	**NE**
is implicitly contradicted or implicitly refuted in the text	**IC**
is explicitly contradicted or refuted in the text.	**EC**

(Continued)

(Continued)

Put the appropriate code in the box alongside each statement.

(In the computerised test you will be asked to drag the code to the appropriate answer.)

The views of trainee teachers are not being sought at this stage.

Many trainee teachers feel they have not been fully prepared with the essential practical skills for teaching.

Inspection helps to raise standards and ensure that the best training is given.

Some new teachers are not as good at managing behaviour as they should be.

The present system for the selection of trainees is satisfactory.

Selecting headings and subheadings

From the four options below, choose the most suitable subheading for the second half of the text to be inserted at the top of paragraph 5. Tick the box next to your choice of subheading.

(In the computerised test you will be asked to drag a tick to your choice of answer.)

☐ Selecting for quality

☑ Going from strength to strength

☐ Need for a fresh focus

☐ Calling all teachers

Identifying possible readership or audience for a text

From the list of possible audiences for this document, select the audience that you think it would be most relevant to, and put an **M** in the box alongside; and the one you think it would be least relevant to, and put an **L** in the box alongside.

*(In the computerised test you will be asked to drag an **M** for the most relevant audience, or an **L** for the least relevant audience, into the appropriate boxes.)*

☐ Headteachers in primary schools

☐ Teaching staff in a university school of education

☐ Teachers of English in primary schools

☐ Qualified teachers working in schools

Remember: only three of these nine aspects of literacy will appear in the actual test.

5 | Literacy skills practice test

Introduction

The Literacy Skills Test is conducted online as described in the Introduction section of this book, 'What is the test like?' (see page 1). This paper-based practice test simulates the Literacy Skills Test as closely as possible.

In the Literacy Skills Test the Spelling section is audio based; however, this version is modelled on the hearing impaired multiple-choice format available in the Literacy Skills Test. The Spelling section only tests your ability to spell; punctuation, grammar and comprehension are not assessed. In the Literacy Skills Test, the Spelling section must be completed first; you cannot then return to it. The remaining sections can be completed in any order.

The Punctuation, Grammar and Comprehension questions in this practice test use close adaptations of the rubric from the Literacy Skills Test.

The Punctuation passage is already partly punctuated. As in the actual test, you are expected to supply any missing punctuation in a way that is consistent with the existing punctuation. There are 15 points where punctuation needs to be inserted. There may be other points where punctuation could be correctly inserted, even though it may not be strictly necessary. You will not gain marks for these unnecessary insertions nor will any marks be deducted.

In this paper-based version add punctuation in the space below the point in the text where you think it is needed. Include the word or adjacent words involved with the punctuation.

> **REMEMBER:**
>
> **You are not required to remove or rewrite any sections of the passage; just insert punctuation.**

The Grammar and Comprehension questions are all 'tick-box' forms of multiple-choice questions. You will not be required to write any text.

> **REMEMBER:**
>
> - **Not all 12 items of punctuation, 23 points of grammar or 9 comprehension question types appear in any one test.**
> - **Any one test will only sample the test specification.**
> - **The total mark for the test is between 48 and 50 marks.**
> - **The pass threshold is 63%.**
> - **This following test carries 49 marks; you will need a score of 30 marks or more to pass.**

LITERACY SKILLS PRACTICE TEST

READ THE INSTRUCTIONS CAREFULLY BEFORE YOU START

There are four sections to this test: Spelling, Punctuation, Grammar and Comprehension. Complete the Spelling section FIRST; do not return to this section during the test.

You have 45 minutes to complete all four sections.

Marking grid

Section	Marks available	Your score	Total
Spelling	10	_____	_____
Punctuation	15	_____	_____
Grammar	12	_____	_____
Comprehension	12	_____	_____

Spelling

Select the correctly spelled word from the box of alternatives. Write your answer in the space in the sentence.

1. The _____ effect of all her hard work was evident at the school concert.

accumolative
accumulative ✓
accumuletive
accumulitive

2. _____ scores enabled comparisons on tests between different groups of pupils.

Standerdised
Standardised
Standedised
Standadised

3. Pupils were requested to return the completed _____ in the envelopes provided.

questionaires ✓
questionnaires
questionnares
questonaires

4. Training aimed to enhance language skills and develop _____ understanding.

> pedergogical
> pedagogicle
> pedegogical
> pedagogical ✓

5. The effectiveness of the locally agreed _____ for religious education was encouraging.

> syllerbus
> syllabus ✓
> syllubus
> sylabus

6. London _____ is an extra allowance paid to teachers working in London.

> wieghting
> waighting
> waiting
> weighting ✓

7. The survey showed that parents felt comfortable conversing with teaching _____.

> personnal
> personal
> personel ✓
> personnel

8. With some boys an inverse culture is a _____ to academic success.

> deterence
> deterrance
> deterance
> deterrence ✓

(Continued)

(Continued)

9. The school swimming pool was closed for routine _____ work.

> maintainance
> maintenance ✓
> mainternance
> maintenence

10. The class is not a _____ group; each pupil has unique and individual needs.

> hermogenous
> homogernous
> homogenus
> homogenous ✓

Punctuation

Correct 15 punctuation omissions in the passage below.

Do not delete or change any of the text; you need only to add punctuation.

Add punctuation in the space below the point in the text where you think it is needed. Include the word or adjacent words involved.

Is television really being pushed aside ?
_____

The 'Childwise Monitor Report (CMR is an annual report on childrens media
_____

consumption. The report found that the number of children with televisions in their
_____

bedroom is falling. The rising trend in the use of gadgets, according to the report
_____

from childwise is the growth in internet use through mobile phones. "Its true that
_____

children use their mobiles for an average of nearly 2 hours a day," said a researcher
_____

however the multi-tasking talents of teenagers mean that many youngsters using
_____

their phones, the internet, or playing on a games console, are often watching
_____

television at the same time." Key findings from the report include 61% of seven to

sixteen year-olds have a mobile phone with internet access; before school, pupils

are more likely to play with their mobiles than watch television after school activities are

more likely to involve the internet than the television; reading at home is more likely to be

from a screen rather than a book; in bed at night, the mobile phone is used by 32% of

children aged five to sixteen.

Grammar

Complete the following passages. At the points where there are blank lines select the best of the given alternatives from the box below. When you have finished, read through the passage to check that you have made the best choices possible.

Grammar Task A
This is a part of a note to parents and carers about a book scheme for the school library.

Dear Parents and Carers,

Last year we ran our first 'Give-A-Book' scheme to celebrate World Book Day.

A	The scheme was so successful, with over 150 books being given to the school, so that we will be running the event again.
B	The scheme was so successful, with over 150 books being given to the school, that we will be running the event again.
C	The scheme was successful, with over 150 books being given to the school, that we will be running the event again.
D	The scheme was that successful, with over 150 books being given to the school, so that we will be running the event again.

(Continued)

(Continued)

A	This year we will be inviting donations in the hope that the scheme was
B	This year we invited donations in the hope that the scheme is
C	This year we are inviting donations in the hope that the scheme will be
D	This year we have invited donations in the hope that the scheme has been

as successful as last year. The book can either be a nearly new book from home or bought from our personalised list available at www.amazon.co.uk (for details, see overleaf). The list of books on Amazon

A	have been compiled by the school.
B	was compiled by the school.
C	are compiled by the school.
D	were compiled by the school.

All donated books

A	should of been selected
B	could have selected
C	could of been selected
D	should have been selected

for use at either KS1 or KS2. To personalise your donated book

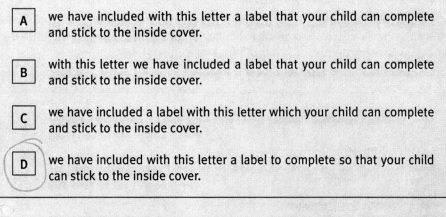

A	we have included with this letter a label that your child can complete and stick to the inside cover.
B	with this letter we have included a label that your child can complete and stick to the inside cover.
C	we have included a label with this letter which your child can complete and stick to the inside cover.
D	we have included with this letter a label to complete so that your child can stick to the inside cover.

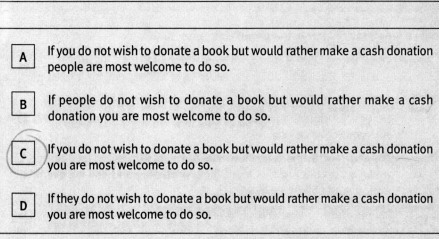

A	If you do not wish to donate a book but would rather make a cash donation people are most welcome to do so.
B	If people do not wish to donate a book but would rather make a cash donation you are most welcome to do so.
C	If you do not wish to donate a book but would rather make a cash donation you are most welcome to do so.
D	If they do not wish to donate a book but would rather make a cash donation you are most welcome to do so.

Please place any cash donations in an envelope marked 'Give A Book' and hand it in at the School Office.

Yours sincerely,

Mrs Clare Thomson
Headteacher

Grammar Task B
This is an extract from a leaflet for parents about a school's homework plan

How to help your child develop basic learning skills at primary school

Helping your child with maths.

(Continued)

(Continued)

Above all, you want your child to discover how pleasurable learning can be. If you're both enjoying an activity, explore all the opportunities it may have to offer. Try to find new ways to enjoy maths with your child. Games, puzzles and jigsaws:

A	these kinds of activity
B	this kind of activities
C	these kinds of activities
D	this kinds of activity

can be a great way to start helping your child with maths.

A	It's important to discover how maths is used in everyday life and to involve your child in this identifying problems and solving them will develop your child's skills.
B	It's important to discover how maths is used in everyday life and to involve your child. In this identifying problems and solving them will develop your child's skills.
C	It's important to discover. How maths is used in everyday life and to involve your child in this identifying problems and solving them will develop your child's skills.
D	It's important to discover how maths is used in everyday life and to involve your child in this. Identifying problems and solving them will develop your child's skills.

If you see him or her puzzling over something, talk about the problem and try to work out the solution together.

A	Just chill out
B	Don't get too anxious
C	Just stay cool
D	Don't get in a stress

if you didn't really enjoy maths yourself at school; times have changed and the subject is now

A	taught very differently than
B	taught very differently from
C	taught very differently over
D	taught very differently before

even a few years ago. Remember, your child can be positively or negatively

A	affected
B	effective
C	effected
D	affective

by your reaction to the situation. When encouraging your child to enjoy maths it might be useful to:

- _____

- _____

- _____

- _____

A
- pointing out the different shapes found around your home
- talking about the quantities of things you buy when shopping together
- letting your child handle money and work out how much things cost
- looking together for numbers on street signs or car registration plates.

(Continued)

(Continued)

B
- point out the different shapes found around your home
- talk about the quantities of things you buy when shopping together
- and let your child handle money and work out how much things cost
- look together for numbers on street signs or car registration plates.

C
- point out the different shapes found around your home
- talk about the quantities of things you buy when shopping together
- let your child handle money and work out how much things cost
- look together for numbers on street signs or car registration plates.

D
- you could point out the different shapes found around your home
- talk about the quantities of things you buy when shopping together
- let your child handle money and work out how much things cost
- look together for numbers on street signs or car registration plates.

Above all, remember to have fun with maths.

Comprehension

Read the following extract from an article about behaviour in schools and complete tasks A, B and C.

Restorative justice in schools
The issue of how to manage disruptive classroom behaviour and unruly pupils has been a perennial feature of the teaching landscape for as long as there have been schools. From the classrooms of Fielding's 'Mr Thwackum' and Dickens's 'Mr M'Choakumchild', to those of A.S. Neill's Summerhill School, teachers have swung from the extremes of 'punitive just-deserts' to the 'libertarian renunciation of discipline'. And all the time successive polls assessing public perception of education continue to cite 'problems with classroom behaviour management' as a major issue. Between the libertarian 'rehabilitation' approach and the 'punitive just-deserts' approach, there are no 'quick-fixes' or 'miracle cures'; the former values an idealised compassion, while the latter values accountability, plus a degree of retribution. Both approaches aim to achieve the same goal: behavioural change in the offender and schools that are safe for all. Evidence is mixed and opinion divided over what works best.

However, practitioners of a restorative justice approach are demonstrating that it is possible to successfully incorporate both compassion and accountability in an approach to managing classroom behaviour and school discipline. Restorative justice can be defined by its fundamental principle: 'When one person has harmed another, the most useful response is to try to repair the harm done.' This approach redefines behaviour problems primarily as 'harmful or damaging' rather than 'law or rule-breaking'. Restorative justice in schools aims to reduce bullying, conflicts and truanting. So far, evidence indicates that it is a particularly promising approach. In practice the methodology revolves around mediation sessions, where pupils are brought face-to-face, perpetrator and victim, to talk about their feelings and the consequences of the actions that have taken place. Trained mediators can be teachers or pupils. Peer mediation involves pupils assisting in resolving less serious incidents and can be particularly effective. In mediation both sides may be asked to verbally agree a contract to avoid a recurrence of similar conflicts. Some sessions can involve large groups of friends after disputes have escalated unchecked beyond the original argument. Conferences can be used for the most serious incidents to reduce the use of exclusions or, when exclusions cannot be avoided, to support the successful reintegration of the excluded pupil.

One school trialling restorative justice trained eight staff to act as mediators. The Behaviour Support Manager said: 'One of the areas where it is making a difference is in reducing bullying. We have yet to have a case where it hasn't worked. It gives pupils the time to reflect on what has happened and how it made them feel. They become responsible for their actions.' Other incidents which triggered restorative intervention included: brawls on the playing field; bullying issues; misbehaviour in lessons; or pushing and shoving in the school corridors. But the technique was also deployed to help friends who had fallen out, or to smooth over rifts sparked by comments on social messaging sites. In some cases, being referred for mediation was an alternative to suspension or detention.

Ofsted's published inspections have recognised the value of adopting this approach. Findings across five recent research studies – in Scotland, Hull, Cardiff, Bristol and London – show that restorative practice in schools reduced exclusion and bullying, and increased attendance and teacher confidence:

> Pupils value the restorative practices that help them understand right and wrong and encourage them to modify behaviour and take responsibility for their actions.
>
> Ofsted report

A recent DfE report showed that 97% of teachers see restorative practice as the most effective approach to prevent, and deal with, bullying.

> '... developing a restorative ethos and culture that supports the development of social and emotional skills' and 'the adult modelling of positive relationships and communication' were given the highest rating of effectiveness in preventing bullying.
>
> The use and effectiveness of anti-bullying strategies in schools, Report by Goldsmiths, University of London, published by the DfE.

Since a national evaluation, Restorative Justice in Schools, numerous headteachers have chosen to implement its use in their schools. In one London borough, 16 primary schools were trained in restorative justice. An evaluation by the local authority then compared these schools with non-practising schools and found a reduction in exclusions of 51% in the 16 trained schools, in addition to a 65% increase in exclusions in the 32 borough primary schools that had not implemented restorative justice. They also found increased confidence among school staff to deal with bullying and conflicts

(Continued)

(Continued)

in the 16 schools. An independent evaluation in Bristol schools found that restorative justice improved school attendance and reduced exclusion rates. For example, one school used to have around 300 permanent exclusions every year. Since introducing restorative justice three years ago, this has fallen year on year; this year there has been just one permanent exclusion. In Hull, a two-year pilot involved staff from twelve primary and two secondary schools. Evaluation of the schools revealed 73% fewer classroom exclusions, 81% fewer fixed-term exclusion days, and a reduction in instances of verbal abuse between pupils and towards staff of over 70%.

Comprehension Task A
Read the statements below and decide which refer to:

T	Teachers
P	The Public
RJ	Restorative Justice
H	Headteachers
O	Ofsted

Put the correct code in the box to the left of each statement.

Their observation is that behaviour management is a major issue in class.

Following general appraisal, they have elected to use restorative justice.

The aim is to reduce victimisation, fights and absenteeism.

They have always been aware of the issues surrounding classroom behaviour.

They have publicly acknowledged the value of implementing this approach.

Comprehension Task B
From the list below, select the four points that most accurately describe the nature of restorative justice.

It defines behaviour problems as damaging not disobedient and prompts the offender to accept liability and repair the damage.

It confronts face-to-face the problems that arise when pupils ignore the basic rules of classroom behaviour.

It encompasses both 'empathy' and 'liability for consequences' when dealing with unacceptable classroom behaviour.

☐ It abandons more libertarian views in favour of taking responsibility for seeing that the punishment fits the crime.

☐ Its technique of person-to-person reconciliation, followed by compromise on offending behaviour, eventually reduces disruption.

☐ It involves mediation between 'offender' and 'offended against' to discuss the affects and effects of events that have taken place.

☐ It has the ability to restore teachers' confidence so that they can quickly regain control over classroom behaviour.

☐ Its process of mediation enables many pupils to take responsibility for their actions and so change their behaviour.

☐ It calls the offender to account, making them responsible for compensating the victim and reinstating any losses.

Comprehension Task C
Identifying the meanings of words and phrases

Select the most suitable alternative for the phrase as it appears in the context of the passage. Tick the box next to your choice.

'... has been a perennial feature of the teaching landscape'

(paragraph 1) is closest in meaning to:

| A | has been viewed as an insurmountable problem for teachers |

| B | has always been a familiar topic in the world of education |

| C | has occasionally been the focus of intense pedagogic discussion |

| D | has frequently been ignored as a serious teaching problem |

'... to the libertarian renunciation of discipline.'

(paragraph 1) is closest in meaning to:

| A | to supporting agreed behaviour boundaries. |

| B | to an open-minded tolerance of school rules. |

| C | to a surrender of authority in favour of free will. |

| D | to the abdication of democratic control. |

(Continued)

(Continued)

'... to support the successful reintegration of the excluded pupil.'

(paragraph 2) is closest in meaning to:

A | to maintain the continuing education of the excluded pupil.

B | to make the pupil's return to school as constructive as possible.

C | to give positive guidance on how to control their behaviour in school.

D | to help the pupil settle successfully into their new school.

Spelling

1. *independent*

> **Key points**
>
> Most words that end with that sound end in *-ent.*

2. *demonstrable*

> **Key points**
>
> Some words, like *demonstrate, educate,* lose an element when they gain a suffix.

3. *assessment*

> **Key points**
>
> Words vary in the way that they spell the *s* sound. This word has two pairs of doubles.

4. *adolescence*

> **Key points**
>
> Words vary in the way they spell the *s* sound. This word uses *sc.*

5. *pursue*

> **Key points**
>
> The sound represented here by *ur* is represented by different letter-strings in other words. They simply have to be learned by heart.

6. *fairies*

Key points

Luckily, this is one of the most reliable rules. Nouns that end in a consonant and *-y*, such as *fairy*, *party*, etc., drop the *y* and add *-ies* in the plural form.

7. *weighing*

Key points

This is clear but complex. If the sound is *ee*, the rule for using *i* and *e* together really is '*ie* except after *c*'. If the sound is not *ee*, the *e* comes first.

8. *fuelled*

Key points

Verbs that end in a single *-l*, like *instil*, take a second *l* when either *-ed* or *-ing* is added.

9. *affected*

Key points

The distinction between *affect* and *effect* baffles many educated adults. If you *affect* something, you have an *effect* on it. Try that as a mnemonic, with the *a* of *affect* coming first, as in the alphabet.

10. *responsibility*

Key points

Another case of having to learn by heart. There are just two ways to spell the suffixes we find in *capable* and *terrible*. Of *-oble/ible* and *obility/ibility*, *able/ability* is the more common.

11. *practice*

Key points

Practice/practise and *advice/advise* confuse a lot of us. The words ending in *-ice* are nouns and could have the word *the* before them; the words ending in *-ise* are verbs and could have the word *I* in front of them.

12. *disappear*

> **Key points**
>
> Morphology, the way that words are built up from their parts, helps here. The prefixes *mis-* and *dis-* end in a single *-s*. What follows is a stem word, like *-take* or *-appear*. Those who write *dissappear* have imagined a non-existent prefix *diss-*.

13. *possession*

> **Key points**
>
> Here, the sound *s* is represented twice by *ss*. The double *ss* is very likely in the middle of a word and quite likely at the end.

14. *impracticable*

> **Key points**
>
> This is a mixture of morphology and the need to learn by heart whether a word uses *-able* or *-ible*. The morphology involved is a series of prefix + stem + suffix: *im + practice + able*. *Practice* loses *e*; *able* changes.

15. *humorous*

> **Key points**
>
> The stem word, the abstract noun *humour*, drops the *u* when it adds the adjective suffix *-ous*. This happens in other words, such as *labour, laborious* (but notice the added *i* in *laborious*).

16. *exaggerated*

> **Key points**
>
> Remember that the commonest type of misspelling is the use or non-use of the double consonant (incidentally, notice that word *misspelling*). This is one of the hardest to remember because there are no analogies.

17. *regrettably*

> **Key points**
>
> This is not about *oble/ible* but about the way that a verb that ends in a consonant such as tis likely to double that consonant when an adverb suffix, such as *-ably*, is added. There are also analogies with *forget, forgettably*.

18. *automatically*

> **Key points**
>
> Apart from the use of a Greek suffix, *auto-*, meaning *self*, it is also a case of a fairly long and complex word whose spelling is close to the way it is said.

19. *curriculum*

> **Key points**
>
> Another example of the double consonant; these words are best learned by heart.

20. *embarrassment*

> **Key points**
>
> A useful mnemonic with this word might be: He went Really Red and Smiled Shyly with embaRRaSSment.

21. *pedagogy*

> **Key points**
>
> Meaning 'the science of teaching'. The origin is Greek: 'paidagagos' – the slave who took children to and from school. This is a spelling best learned by heart.

22. *allowed*

> **Key points**
>
> Confusion between such homophones as *allowed*, *a loud* and *aloud* is serious because it shows that the writer does very little reading and that the simple grammatical and meaning distinctions between the participle *allowed* and the adverb *aloud* have been overlooked.

23. *allot*

> **Key points**
>
> The words *allot* and *a lot* are also homophones; they sound the same as each other but have different meanings. We *allot* when we distribute something among recipients. There may be *a lot* of recipients.

24. *maturity*

Key points

It is another example of the way that an adjective, *mature,* drops the final *e* when the noun suffix *-ity* is added but it is also quite regular phonically.

25. *counselling*

Key points

The usual UK spelling is 'counselling'. While the US version, 'counseling', is acceptable, the misspellings in the question (counciling, counsiling, councelling) are incorrect. Most errors arise from the confusion of the words 'council' and 'counsel'.

26. *miscellaneous*

Key points

Notice the use of *sc* for the *s* sound, the double *ll* and the *e* in the final syllable. Also, its parts are *misc + ell + an + eous.*

27. *approximation*

Key points

The use of a double consonant is a frequent problem; the use of *x* is infrequent.

28. *reprehensible*

Key points

There are no double consonants but the use of *i* in the final consonant is fairly rare.

29. *apprenticeship*

Key points

Here, there is a double consonant; the *s* sound is represented by *ce.*

Punctuation

1. As soon as we speak, (1) we reveal a great deal of ourselves to our audience. Suppose you ask someone,

   (2) "Shall we have a drink? (3)" (4)

   Suppose the other person replies, (5)

   "Yes, I'd like a whiskey, (6) me."

   That tag, *me*, tells you that the speaker probably comes from (7) Manchester.

   Sometimes, what people say does tell you something about their origin but it is less definite. A friend asks you and another friend,

   "Now, what would youse two like to drink?"

   The questioner may or may not come from Ireland but will certainly have a background there because that use of (8) 'youse', unknown in Standard English, has its roots in the Irish having one form of 'you' for one person (9) (tú) and another form of 'you' for two people (9) (sibh). However, (10) none of this means that any of these speakers could actually speak any Irish!

Key points

   (1) The subordinate clause appears first so it should be separated from the main clause by a comma.

   (2) The first letter in the sentence needs a capital letter.

   (3) A question requires a question mark.

   (4) Direct speech needs speech marks both at the beginning and at the end. The two marks, paired, form a consistency.

   (5) The mark before a direct quotation is usually a comma.

   (6) A comma is needed to separate the tag 'me' from the rest.

   (7) The city of Manchester requires a capital letter.

   (8) This is a bit of language that differs from the rest of the text and needs quotation marks to identify it.

   (9) The Irish words tú and sibh break into the rest and are best placed within brackets.

   (10) A comma is needed after 'However'. This is important because 'however' can have two different meanings:

   – nevertheless; yet; on the other hand; in spite of that

   – to whatever extent or degree; no matter how

The comma indicates the intended meaning. Consider the two sets of sentences below:

However the scripts were analysed, the marks remained the same.

However, the scripts were analysed; the marks remained the same.

Or

The marks remained the same however the scripts were analysed.

The marks remained the same; however, the scripts were analysed.

2. The concern of the (11) Head of (12) English was evident after reading the (13) 'Can do Better' report on literacy. If we look at (14) boys' performance in English, we have to agree that there is, generally (15), some cause for concern. Is there anything that can be done to help them improve?

Among the (16) short-term approaches that seemed to help boys are (17):

enthusiastically encouraged private reading;

clearly set tasks (18);

explicit teaching of reading strategies;

a wide range of outcomes from reading;

reading preferences that are discussed.

Key points

(11) and (12) As proper nouns, the head of english needs capital letters: 'Head of English'.

(13) The title of a document should be in single quotation marks.

(14) The performance belongs to the boys so an apostrophe is needed after the s.

(15) The interruption of the flow of the sentence by the word 'generally' should be marked by twinned commas, one before and one after the word.

(16) A hyphen should be used to link the two words to show they are one unit of meaning. Without a hyphen 'short term' could mean a school term of only a few weeks.

(17) A list is being introduced so a colon is necessary.

(18) Each item on the list is more than one word long and needs separating with a semicolon.

3. What is it about (19) Standard English that makes it standard? (20)

(21)

Like every language, English has gone through many changes. The Saxons and Angles who settled here brought their own languages with them, (22) predominantly Saxon, and after a while the dialects of Anglo-Saxon overcame the Celtic languages that had flourished along with Latin until soon after the Romans left in 410AD. The languages spoken by the later Scandinavian invaders were probably just about intelligible to some of the Anglo-(23)Saxons but changes and borrowings continued: the new invaders' (24) legacy to us includes *they, them, their*. Anglo-Saxon, modified by Scandinavian, with dialects that were barely intelligible to other Anglo-Saxon speakers, continued for hundreds of years but, thankfully, (25) it became simpler. (26) The German word for *big* is *gross* but it has six versions. Our Anglo-Saxon ancestors had eleven versions of adjectives; (27) we have just three: *big, bigger, biggest*. Even when we complicate matters by having *good, better,* (28) **best**, that is still easier than Anglo-Saxon! (29)

Key points

(19) There is no need for a capital for *standard*; the lower case version is now the accepted convention.

(20) A question requires a question mark.

(21) After the first sentence, comes the beginning of an answer. A new paragraph is needed.

(22) *predominantly Saxon* breaks into the sentence and needs a pair of commas, one before and one after.

(23) A hyphen is needed for Anglo-Saxon (as for Irish-American).

(24) The noun is *invaders* so they need an apostrophe before *legacy*.

(25) *Thankfully* is also an interruption and a pair of commas is needed.

(26) A sentence ends with a full stop.

(27) There are two sentences but their meanings are so closely related that they need a semicolon to link them.

(28) The series of three items in a list without an *and* requires a series of commas.

(29) This is an exclamation but that shows how personal punctuation is.

Grammar

Unrelated participles

A 2 *Vygotsky* is the one who did the *realising*; who *realised*.
B 1 The *headteacher* was the one who was *persuaded*.
C 2 It was *Peters* who *conceded*, who did the *conceding*, not his views.
D 4 The *children were thought*, nobody and nothing else.

> ### Key points
>
> This relates to the issue of agreement between subject and verb. You clarify the matter by asking *who did* it.

Wrong tense or tense consistency

A 2

> ### Key points
>
> *have been* makes most sense because it matches or agrees with the other verbs: the series of *wish* and *had worked* followed by *was* and *has meant*. *Made* confirms the choice of *have been* because it makes *was* impossible.

B 4

> ### Key points
>
> When there are several verbs in a sentence, some in different tenses, the question is to decide what other verb this one should be like. This verb is part of a series beginning *I'll make* and so is in the future tense.

C 1

> ### Key points
>
> There is a series of short clauses beginning with *I can't* and all have to use the same verb form.

D 4

> **Key points**
>
> *grown* makes most sense because it is the only option that fits the use of the verb form *have examined*: *compared* parallels *grown* because the two verbs make use of the *have* of *have examined*.

Lack of agreement between subject and verb

A 4

> **Key points**
>
> The subject of the sentence is *trouble*, a singular noun, so the verb has to be singular also: *is*. There can often be a problem with subjects whose headwords are a long way from the verb; it is very easy to be trapped into picking up the nearest noun and thinking that that is the subject (in this sentence, the trap is *way*). This question does also ask you to be careful about the tense: the present.

B 2

> **Key points**
>
> The subject is *attitudes* so the verb has to be in the plural: *were*. Again, there is always a problem with a sentence with several nouns: out of *friend, cause, problem, attitudes, teacher*, which is the subject of this verb? The correct tense confirms the answer.

C 3

> **Key points**
>
> This seems quite easy but the issue is that there are, apparently, several subjects: *teacher, sicknesses, parents*. The clue is the word *or* which tells you, logically, that only one thing is the subject, not everything listed. This is confirmed by the singular *it*.

D 3

> **Key points**
>
> This time, the tense not only fits the grammar but also the obvious sense of *the future*.

Comprehension

Attributing statements to categories

| O | They are going to require more from teacher training courses.

Key points

Para 1 says that Ofsted is proposing to raise expectations of providers of teacher training.

| HMCI | They regard the training of the next cohort of teachers as very significant.

Key points

Para 3 reports the HMCI saying that the training of the next generation of teachers is crucial.

| TT | They are going to be expected to know how to develop literacy skills.

Key points

Para 5 says that inspections will focus even more on the quality of training and trainees' subject knowledge and their understanding and competence in developing pupils' literacy skills.

| ITEP | They are going to have to look more closely at placements.

Key points

Para 5 says that inspection will concentrate on the quality of partnerships ITE providers have with settings, schools and colleges.

Completing a bulleted list

It is anticipated that all future ITE inspections will:

take account of the views of newly or recently qualified teachers

> ### Key points
>
> Bullet point 3 says Ofsted proposes to take account of the views of users, trainees and former trainees, including newly qualified and recently qualified teachers

target inspections only where improvement is most needed

> ### Key points
>
> Para 6 says Ofsted proposes that future inspections will be informed by a robust risk assessment process so they can be targeted where improvement is needed most.

improve ITE by providing an external evaluation of strengths and weaknesses

> ### Key points
>
> Bullet point 9 says that Ofsted proposes to drive improvement in the sector by providing an external evaluation of strengths and weaknesses.

Sequencing information

FIRST Partnerships previously judged to be satisfactory will be inspected.

> ### Key points
>
> This is the first part of the new proportionate process described in paragraph 6.

SECOND Those that continue to be satisfactory will be inspected within 12 to 18 months.

> ### Key points
>
> This is the next step in the process.

THIRD Partnerships will have a full inspection within three years of a previous inspection.

> ### Key points
>
> This is the final stage of the new process.

Presenting main points

Upgrade the quality of training given by ITE providers.

> **Key points**
>
> Para 1 says that Ofsted is proposing to raise expectations of providers of teacher training.

Look more closely at how trainees are evaluated and selected for ITE.

> **Key points**
>
> Para 5 says that Ofsted proposes that inspection will look more closely at the selection of trainees.

Ensure practical teaching skills are top of the agenda for trainees.

> **Key points**
>
> Para 1 says that Ofsted is proposing to ensure that more trainees are better prepared with the practical skills that teachers need most. The point (about behaviour management) is then repeated three times elsewhere in the text.

Introduce one comprehensive criterion for the general effectiveness of ITE provision.

> **Key points**
>
> Para 2 says that clearer, more challenging criteria with fewer, more streamlined judgements and one overarching judgement for overall effectiveness are to be drawn up.

These points should **not** be included:

Encourage teachers working in schools to tell them their views on ITE.

> **Key points**
>
> Para 4 says HMCI would like 'in particular those who provide training, are currently in training, or thinking of joining a teacher training programme, to tell us their views'. This list does not include practising teachers.

Gauge the effectiveness of the teaching of phonics by newly qualified teachers.

Key points

Bullet point 6 suggests that inspections will look at the provision of phonics training received by trainees where their feedback raises concerns.

Introduce a thematic approach into the inspection of behaviour management.

Key points

Para 5 talks about a thematic element to inspection; not just about the inspection of behaviour management.

Scrutinise the inspection criteria used to assess teachers in schools.

Key points

The document concerns the scrutiny of teaching in ITE, not the teaching in schools.

Reduce the notice period given prior to inspection of ITE provision.

Key points

This is not a main objective; it is a topic on which Ofsted is seeking views.

Matching texts to summaries

Reread paragraphs 1, 3 and 5. From the list of statements below, select the one that most accurately summarises the content of these three paragraphs. Tick the box next to your choice. (*In the computerised test you will be asked to drag a tick symbol to the box beside your choice.*)

The most important attributes of the trainee teacher emerging from ITE are the abilities to control and manage behaviour and to teach literacy effectively.

Key points

When summarising the three paragraphs look for the key points they share. All three stress the importance of being able to manage behaviour and to teach literacy.

While the other statements are significant, they are not common to all three paragraphs and should not be chosen.

Identifying the meanings of words and phrases

'... raise expectations of providers of teacher training' (paragraph 1) is closest in meaning to:

investigate the endeavours of providers of teacher training

Key points

This is only a part of raising expectations. **Do not** choose this option.

lift the requirements of providers of teacher training

Key points

In this context 'requirements' and 'expectations' are very close in meaning. **This option should be selected.**

boost the hopes of providers of teacher training

Key points

In this context, 'boosting hopes' is not the same thing as 'raising expectations'. **Do not** choose this option.

increase the demands on providers of teacher training

Key points

Increasing demands is not the same thing as raising expectations; it is the result of raising expectations. **Do not** choose this option.

'... a more proportionate approach to' (paragraph 6) is closest in meaning to:

a more commensurate method of

Key points

The words 'commensurate' and 'proportionate' have a very similar meaning, i.e. that of 'balance' or 'equality' or 'levelness'. **This option should be selected.**

a more detached pathway to

> **Key points**
>
> The words 'detached' and 'proportionate' do not have the same meaning. **Do not** choose this option.

a more competitive move towards

> **Key points**
>
> In this context there is no defined competitor for inspection and this option should not be chosen. **Do not** choose this option.

a more rigorous course of

> **Key points**
>
> This means a tougher course of inspection; this does not have the same meaning as 'balanced' or 'in proportion'. **Do not** choose this option.

Evaluating statements about the text

| EC | The views of trainee teachers are not being sought at this stage. |

> **Key points**
>
> Paragraph 4 states: 'I'd like to encourage anyone ... in particular ... those who are currently in training, ... to tell us their views.'

| NE | Many trainee teachers feel they have not been fully prepared with the essential practical skills for teaching. |

> **Key points**
>
> This does not appear in the text.

| S | Inspection helps to raise standards and ensure that the best training is given. |

Key points

Paragraph 4 says that inspection helps to raise standards and ensure the best training is provided.

| I | Some new teachers are not as good at managing behaviour as they should be. |

Key points

In four places the document states that classroom behaviour and management are issues that need to be addressed with a view to improvement. This implies that in some newly qualified teachers, these skills are lacking.

| IC | The present system for the selection of trainees is satisfactory. |

Key points

Paragraph 5 opening sentence 'it is proposed that inspection will look more closely at the selection of trainees ...' Without actually saying as much, this contradicts the idea that the current system is satisfactory.

Selecting headings and subheadings

Selecting for quality

Key points

This is one of a number of important points in this section of the text. **Do not** choose it.

Going from strength to strength

Key points

This covers 'building on the strengths' (paragraph 5); 'retain the focus on trainees' outcomes'; continue to involve leaders et al. in inspections; and continue to drive improvement (bullet points). **This option should be selected.**

Need for a fresh focus

Key points

This is one of a number of proposals in the document; further, the need to 'focus afresh' is mentioned in the first half of the document (paragraph 4). **Do not** choose it.

Calling all teachers

Key points

This is a fairly minor point in the document first mentioned in paragraph 4. **Do not** choose it.

Identifying possible readership or audience for a text

Headteachers in primary schools

Key points

These headteachers might be interested but only if they were partnership schools or offering ITE training. **Do not** choose this option.

Teaching staff in a university school of education

Key points

These institutions are likely to be very interested as they are the subject of inspection. **Choose this audience as the 'most relevant' (M).**

Teachers of English in primary schools

Key points

These teachers might be interested especially in the references to literacy and phonics. However, they would not be directly affected by many of the other details. **Do not** choose this option.

Qualified teachers working in schools

Literacy Skills Practice Test

Spelling

1. *accumulative* ✓

2. *Standardised* ✓

3. *questionnaires* ✗

(Continued)

single consonant before a suffix beginning with a vowel when a single vowel precedes the consonant.' While this works for 'question + aire = questionnaire' and 'legion + aire = legionnaire' it doesn't apply to 'million + aire = millionaire' or 'commission + aire = commissionaire'. There are relatively few words ending in -aire; this would be a spelling best learned by heart.

4. *pedagogical* √

Key points

This word derives from the noun 'pedagogy' meaning the art or profession of teaching. (The origin is Greek: 'paidagagos' – the slave who took children to and from school.) This is a spelling best learned by heart.

5. *syllabus* √

Key points

The most common misspelling of syllabus involves the double consonant: 'sylabus'. There are no hard and fast rules about doubling consonants and this is a spelling best learned by heart.

6. *weighting* √

Key points

All spelling rules have exceptions. The well-known rule 'i before e except after c' is a useful reminder provided that you memorise the exceptions; 'weight' is one of them and is a spelling best learned by heart.

7. *personnel* ✗

Key points

Over half of the misspellings of this word involve not doubling the 'n', and a quarter involve doubling the 'l' unnecessarily. A useful tip may be to remember that the root word 'person' is formed from the French 'personne', which is always spelled with a double 'n'. Errors are also sometimes made when 'personnel' is mistaken for the similar sounding word 'personal', which has a different meaning.

8. deterrence

Key points

The root word here is the verb 'deter'. The suffix -ence is added to form the noun 'deterrence'. There are no hard and fast rules about doubling the 'r'. For example, the word 'refer' is not spelled 'referrence' but 'reference'. This is a spelling best learned by heart.

9. maintenance

Key points

The spelling of this word does not follow any rules. Some misspellings arise from the fact that the word is derived from the verb 'maintain', the present form of which is 'maintaining' and it would seem logical that the word would follow this pattern and be spelled 'maintainance'. However, it does not. This is a spelling best learned by heart.

10. homogenous

Key points

This adjective is formed from the two Greek words 'homo' meaning 'the same' and 'genos' meaning 'kind'. It is a spelling that is best learned by heart.

Punctuation

Original passage
Is television really being pushed aside

The 'Childwise Monitor Report (CMR) is an annual report on children's media consumption. The report found that the number of children with televisions in their bedroom is falling. The rising trend in the use of gadgets, according to the report from childwise, is the growth in internet use through mobile phones. "It's true that children use their mobiles for an average of nearly 2 hours a day," said a researcher. however the multi-tasking talents of teenagers mean that many youngsters using their phones, the internet, or playing on a games console, are often watching television at the same time." Key findings from the report include: 61% of seven to sixteen year-olds have a mobile phone with internet access; before school, pupils are more likely to play with their mobiles than watch television. after school activities are more likely to involve the internet than the television; reading at home is more likely to be from a screen rather than a book; in bed at night, the mobile phone is used by 32% of children aged five to sixteen.

Corrected passage
Is television really being pushed aside?

The 'Childwise Monitor Report' (CMR) is an annual report on children's media consumption. The report found that the number of children with televisions in their bedroom is falling. The rising trend in the use of gadgets, according to the report from Childwise, is the growth in internet use through mobile phones. "It's true that children use their mobiles for an average of nearly 2 hours a day," said a researcher. "However, the multi-tasking talents of teenagers mean that many youngsters using their phones, the internet, or playing on a games console, are often watching television at the same time."

Key findings from the report include: 61% of seven to sixteen-year-olds have a mobile phone with internet access; before school, pupils are more likely to play with their mobiles than watch television; after school activities are more likely to involve the internet than the television; reading at home is more likely to be from a screen rather than a book; in bed at night, the mobile phone is used by 32% of children aged five to sixteen.

Key points

Line 1 (1 mark)

A question mark is required at the end of the title. No additional punctuation is needed.

Line 2 (3 marks)

The title, Childwise Monitor Report, starts with single quotation marks and should close with single quotation marks. A single quotation mark is needed at the end of the title.

The abbreviation for the title CMR starts with open brackets and should end with closed brackets. A bracket needs to be added after the abbreviation.

An apostrophe of possession is needed in the word children's to show the media 'belongs' to children.

Lines 3 and 4

No additional punctuation is needed.

Line 5 (3 marks)

The proper noun Childwise needs a capital letter.

The supplementary clause 'according to the report from Childwise' starts with a comma on Line 4 and should close with a comma in order to separate it from the main sentence. A comma is needed after the word Childwise.

The word 'Its' needs an apostrophe of omission to show that this is an abbreviation of 'It is'.

Line 6 (4 marks)

A full stop is needed after the word 'researcher' as this is the end of the sentence.

Opening speech marks are needed before the word 'however' because the closing speech marks present on line 9 indicate that the researcher is still being quoted.

The word 'however' needs to start with a capital letter as this is the start of a new sentence.

The word 'however' needs to be followed by a comma.

Lines 7 and 8

No additional punctuation is needed.

Line 9 (3 marks)

From Line 9 to the end of the passage is one sentence and deals exclusively with the fresh topic of the key findings from the report. As such it justifies the start of a new paragraph starting with the word 'Key'.

From reading through the sense of the text, it can be seen that the semicolons in the next five lines form a list of findings. This should be preceded by a colon. The colon should be inserted after the word 'include'.

A hyphen is needed in the phrase 'sixteen year-olds' to show the three words form one unit of meaning. As this stands it could be read as sixteen children who are one year old.

Line 10

No additional punctuation is needed.

Line 11 (1 mark)

To avoid the confusion of before and after school activities, a semicolon is needed after the word 'television' to mark the start of a separate item on the list.

Lines 12 and 13

No additional punctuation is needed.

Grammar

Grammar task A
Dear Parents and Carers,

Last year we ran our first 'Give-A-Book' scheme to celebrate World Book Day.

B   The scheme was so successful, with over 150 books being given to the school, that we will be running the event again.

C   This year we are inviting donations in the hope that the scheme will be

as successful as last year. The book can either be a nearly new book from home or bought from our personalised list available at www.amazon.co.uk (for details, see over-leaf). The list of books on Amazon

B   was compiled by the school.

All donated books

D   should have been selected

for use at either KS1 or KS2. To personalise your donated book

A   we have included with this letter a label that your child can complete and stick to the inside cover.

C   If you do not wish to donate a book but would rather make a cash donation, you are most welcome to do so.

Please place any cash donations in an envelope marked 'Give A Book' and hand it in at the School Office.

Yours sincerely,

Mrs Clare Thomson
Headteacher

Key points

In the grammar tasks you have to complete the blank spaces in a short text by select-ing one of four given alternatives. Your choice should:

- be grammatically acceptable;
- be free from ambiguity;
- fit in with the context, tone and style of the passage;
- be appropriate for the writer's purpose and audience.

Question 1
This question tests your ability to recognise and avoid inappropriate conjunctions in your professional writing.

Correct answer: B The scheme was so successful, with over 150 books being given to the school, that we will be running the event again.

This option is the correct way to use the conjunctions 'so' and 'that' in order to link cause and effect.

Option A: The scheme was so successful, with over 150 books being given to the school, so that we will be running the event again.

This is incorrect because the second 'so' is redundant.

Option C: The scheme was successful, with over 150 books being given to the school, that we will be running the event again.

This is incorrect because there is no explanation or cause behind the 'that'.

Option D: The scheme was that successful, with over 150 books being given to the school, so that we will be running the event again.

This is incorrect because the first 'that' is added needlessly.

Question 2
This question tests your ability to avoid the wrong tense or tense inconsistency and maintain sense, clarity and freedom from ambiguity.

Correct answer: C This year we are inviting donations in the hope that the scheme will be

This option is correct because the verb 'will be' is consistent with an event taking place in the future.

Option A: This year we will be inviting donations in the hope that the scheme was

This is incorrect because 'was' is the wrong tense for an event that will take place in the future.

Option B: This year we invited donations in the hope that the scheme is

This is incorrect because the verb 'is' relates to the present and not to the future.

Option D: This year we have invited donations in the hope that the scheme has been

This is incorrect because 'has been' relates to the past rather than to the future.

Question 3
This question tests your ability to recognise consistency of agreement between subject and verb within written Standard English.

Correct answer: B was compiled by the school.

This option is correct because the sentence now reads, 'The list of books on Amazon was compiled by the school.' Both the subject and the verb are in agreement.

(Continued)

(Continued)

It is important to consider the whole sentence:

Option A: The list of books on Amazon have been compiled by the school.

Option C: The list of books on Amazon are compiled by the school.

Option D: The list of books on Amazon were compiled by the school.

These options are all incorrect. The subject of the verb is the 'list'. This is singular in that there is only one list. None of the verbs in these options are in agreement.

Question 4
This question tests your ability to recognise consistency within written Standard English when using expressions such as 'could have', 'should have' or 'might have'.

Correct answer: D should have been selected

The correct verb 'have' has been used.

Options A and C are incorrect.

In spoken English expressions such as 'should have' or 'could have' are often shortened and pronounced as 'should've' or 'could've'. Verbally the '-ve' sound is very similar to 'of' and this can often appear erroneously in written work as 'should of'. 'Should of' and could of' do not make sense. The preposition 'of' has at least eight functions; however, it cannot be combined sensibly with modal verbs such as 'would', 'could', 'should' as a substitute for the verb 'to have'.

Option B is also incorrect. Without the word 'been' the sense is that the donated books did the selecting.

Question 5
This question tests your ability to recognise and avoid unrelated participles in your professional writing.

Correct answer: A we have included with this letter a label that your child can complete and stick to the inside cover.

This option is correct because the sentence is constructed so that it makes sense and is free from ambiguity.

Option B is incorrect because it reads as if the book is to be personalised with the letter.

Option C is incorrect because it reads as if the child can complete the letter.

Option D is incorrect because it reads as if the child will stick to the inside cover of the book.

Question 6
This question tests your ability to recognise and avoid a shift in person within a sentence, or across sentences, and so maintain a professionally suitable style of writing.

Correct answer: C If you do not wish to donate a book but would rather make a cash donation you are most welcome to do so.

This option is correct because of the consistent use of the second person, 'you'.

Option A is incorrect because of the combination of 'you' and 'people'.

Option B is incorrect because of the combination of 'people' and 'you'.

Option D is incorrect because of the combination of 'they' and 'you'.

Grammar task B

How to help your child develop basic learning skills at primary school.

Helping your child with maths.

Above all, you want your child to discover how pleasurable learning can be. If you're both enjoying an activity, explore all the opportunities it may have to offer. Try to find new ways to enjoy maths with your child. Games, puzzles and jigsaws;

C   **these kinds of activities**

can be a great way to start helping your child with maths.

D   **It's important to discover how maths is used in everyday life and to involve your child in this. Identifying problems and solving them will develop your child's skills.**

If you see him or her puzzling over something, talk about the problem and try to work out the solution together.

B   **Don't get too anxious**

if you didn't really enjoy maths yourself at school; times have changed and the subject is now

B   **taught very differently from**

even a few years ago. Remember, your child may be positively or negatively

A   **affected**

by your reaction to the situation.

When encouraging your child to enjoy maths, it might be useful to:

C

- point out the different shapes found around your home
- talk about the quantities of things you buy when shopping together
- let your child handle money and work out how much things cost
- look together for numbers on street signs or car registration plates.

Above all, remember to have fun with maths.

Key points

Question 1
This question tests your ability to use determiner/noun agreement consistently within written Standard English.

Correct answer: C these kinds of activities

This is the correct answer because the determiner 'these' agrees with the noun 'activities'; they are both plural.

Option A: these kinds of activity

Option B: this kind of activities

Option D: this kinds of activity

All three options contain a lack of agreement between the determiners (these and this) and the nouns (kind/kinds of activity/activities).

Question 2
This question tests your ability to recognise and observe sentence boundaries consistently within written Standard English.

Correct answer: D It's important to discover how maths is used in everyday life and to involve your child in this. Identifying problems and solving them will develop your child's skills.

Option A is incorrect because there are no sentence boundaries. The sense is lost as two sentences run in together.

Option B is incorrect because the boundary between the sentences is in the wrong place. While the first sentence makes sense, the second is confusing.

Option C is incorrect because, while the first sentence just about makes sense, the second is very confused and meaning is lost.

Question 3
This question tests your ability to use a consistent register and tone when writing for a professional audience.

Correct answer: B Don't get too anxious

Options A, C and D are incorrect because they are too colloquial in tone for a document of this formal nature.

Question 4
This question tests your ability to use prepositions consistently within written Standard English.

Correct answer: B taught very differently from

Options A, C and D are incorrect because the prepositions 'than', 'over' and 'before' either indicate the wrong relationship between the time spans discussed, or alter the meaning of the sentence.

Question 5
This question tests your ability to identify how the confusion of words can affect sense, clarity and freedom from ambiguity in writing.

Correct answer: A affected

In this context 'affected' means 'influenced', which is the correct meaning within the text.

Option B: 'effective' means 'successful in producing a desired or intended result'. In this context it is the parent's reaction that can be effective.

Option C: 'effected' is the past tense of the verb 'effect' which means 'to bring about or cause an event'. In this context this does not make sense.

Option D: 'affective' is an adjective that relates to moods and feelings. In this case it would mean that the child would be able to change behaviour in others at an emotional level. This does not make sense in this context.

Question 6
This question tests your ability to use parallelism in lists within professional writing.

Correct answer: C

When encouraging your child to enjoy maths it might be useful to:

- **point out the different shapes found around your home**
- **talk about the quantities of things you buy when shopping together**

(Continued)

(Continued)

- let your child handle money and work out how much things cost
- look together for numbers on street signs or car registration plates.

This is correct because all the items in the list are grammatically similar. Each item also 'follows on' from the stem to form an independent, grammatically correct sentence.

Options A, B and D all contain one or more items that do not 'follow-on' from the stem to form grammatically correct sentences.

Comprehension

Comprehension task A

| P | Their observation is that behaviour management is a major issue in class.

| H | Following general appraisal, they have elected to use restorative justice.

| RJ | The aim is to reduce victimisation, fights and absenteeism.

| T | They have always been aware of the issues surrounding classroom behaviour.

| O | They have publicly acknowledged the value of implementing this approach. ✓

Key points

This task asks you to attribute statements to their source. The statement might be a quote or a function that should be correctly attached to a person or an organisation. Consider each statement carefully and identify key words or ideas before making your decision:

☐ **Their observation is that behaviour management is a major issue in class.**

Skim read the passage through and ask, 'Who takes the view that behaviour management is a major issue?'

Advice: Read paragraph 1, where you will find the sentence: 'And all the time successive polls assessing public perception of education continue to cite "problems with classroom behaviour management" as a major issue.' It states that public perception sees this as a major issue; therefore the correct answer is P.

☐ **Following general appraisal, they have elected to use restorative justice.**

Skim read the passage through and ask, 'Who decided to put restorative justice into practice after it had been widely considered?'

Advice: Read the beginning of the final paragraph: 'Since a national evaluation, *Restorative Justice in Schools,* numerous headteachers have chosen to implement its use in their schools.' The correct answer is **H**.

☐ **The aim is to reduce victimisation, fights and absenteeism.**

Skim read the passage through and ask, 'Who, or what, is trying to stop harassment, violence and truanting?'

Advice: Read paragraph 2: 'Restorative justice in schools aims to reduce bullying, conflicts and truanting.' The correct answer is **RJ**.

☐ **They have always been aware of the issues surrounding classroom behaviour.**

Skim read the passage through and ask, 'Who have always known about the main aspects of classroom behaviour?'

Advice: Read the first sentence: 'The issue of how to manage disruptive classroom behaviour and unruly pupils has been a perennial feature of the teaching landscape for as long as there have been schools.' The correct answer is **T**.

☐ **They have publicly acknowledged the value of implementing this approach.**

Skim read the passage through and ask, 'Who have openly published their approval of using restorative justice in schools?'

Advice: Read paragraph 4: 'Ofsted's published inspections have recognised the value of adopting this approach.' The correct answer is **O**.

Comprehension task B

☐* It defines behaviour problems as damaging not disobedient and prompts the offender to accept liability and repair the damage.

☐* It encompasses both 'empathy' and 'liability for consequences' when dealing ✓ with unacceptable classroom behaviour.

☐* It involves mediation between 'offender' and 'offended against' to discuss the affects and effects of events that have taken place.

☐* Its process of mediation enables many pupils to take responsibility for their actions and so change their behaviour. ✓

Key points

This task requires you to identify main or key points of information about a topic. You are presented with nine statements. From your reading and comprehension of the passage, you are asked to select the four points that most accurately describe the nature of restorative justice.

Consider each statement carefully and avoid making assumptions.

'It defines behaviour problems as damaging not disobedient and prompts the offender to accept liability and repair the damage.'

Advice: Read paragraph 2: 'When one person has harmed another, the most useful response is to try to repair the harm done'. This approach redefines behaviour problems primarily as 'harmful or damaging' rather than 'law or rule-breaking.' **This option should be chosen.**

'It confronts face-to-face the problems that arise when pupils ignore the basic rules of classroom behaviour.'

This does not accurately describe restorative justice. The text states that it actually plays down this aspect of rule or law breaking and focuses mainly on the aspect of harmful behaviour. This option should **not** be chosen.

'It encompasses both "empathy" and "liability for consequences" when dealing with unacceptable classroom behaviour.'

Advice: Read paragraph 2: 'practitioners of a restorative justice approach are demonstrating that it is possible to successfully incorporate both compassion and accountability.' **This option should be chosen.**

'It abandons more libertarian views in favour of taking responsibility for seeing that the punishment fits the crime.'

There is no evidence in the passage to suggest that restorative justice takes such a punitive approach. This option should **not** be chosen.

'Its technique of person to person reconciliation, followed by compromise on offending behaviour, eventually reduces disruption.'

This option is only partly true. There is no evidence that a compromise is made. This option should **not** be chosen.

'It involves mediation between "offender" and "offended against" to discuss the affects and effects of events that have taken place.'

Advice: Read paragraph 2: 'In practice the methodology revolves around mediation sessions, where pupils are brought face-to-face, perpetrator and victim, to talk about their feelings and the consequences of the actions that have taken place.' **This option should be chosen.**

'It has the ability to restore teachers' confidence so that they can quickly regain control over classroom behaviour.'

While some mention is made of the benefit to teachers' confidence, this is more of a side-effect than a description of the nature of restorative justice. This option should **not** be chosen.

'Its process of mediation enables many pupils to take responsibility for their actions and so change their behaviour.'

Advice: Read the quotation below paragraph 4: 'Pupils value the restorative practices that help them understand right and wrong, and encourage them to modify behaviour and take responsibility for their actions.' **This option should be chosen.**

'It calls the offender to account, making them responsible for compensating the victim and reinstating any losses.'

Retribution is not in the nature of restorative justice. This option should **not** be chosen.

Comprehension task C

'... has been a perennial feature of the teaching landscape'

| B | *has always been a familiar topic in the world of education* ✓ |

'... to the libertarian renunciation of discipline.'

| C | *to a surrender of authority in favour of free will.* ✓ |

'... to support the successful reintegration of the excluded pupil.'

| B | *to make the pupil's return to school as constructive as possible.* |

3/3

Key points

This task requires you to identify the meaning of words or phrases. You are given three phrases taken from the passage. For each phrase you are asked to select the most appropriate replacement from a list of four given options.

Advice: Skim the passage and identify the phrase in context. Carefully read the phrase and surrounding text to make sure you understand the meaning. Remember that you are asked for the best meaning in the context of the passage.

(Continued)

(Continued)

'... has been a perennial feature of the teaching landscape'

(paragraph 1) is closest in meaning to:

Option A: has been viewed as an insurmountable problem for teachers

This means that the poor classroom behaviour is seen as an impossible problem to solve. This is not what is meant in this context and this option should **not** be chosen.

Option B: has always been a familiar topic in the world of education

This means that the issue is well known. This is closest in meaning to the phrase from the text. **This option should be chosen.**

Option C: has occasionally been the focus of intense pedagogic discussion

This means that teachers have occasionally discussed this issue. This is not what is meant in this context and this option should **not** be chosen.

Option D: has frequently been ignored as a serious teaching problem

There is no mention of the problem being ignored and this option should **not** be chosen.

'... to the libertarian renunciation of discipline.'

(paragraph 1) is closest in meaning to:

Option A: to supporting agreed behaviour boundaries.

This means that a certain amount of negotiated discipline is upheld. The phrase from the passage means there will be no discipline at all. This option should **not** be chosen.

Option B: to an open-minded tolerance of school rules.

This means that school rules will be accepted. This is not what is meant by the phrase from the passage and this option should **not** be chosen.

Option C: to a surrender of authority in favour of free will.

This means that there will be complete freedom for pupils with no discipline in place. **This option should be chosen.**

Option D: to the abdication of democratic control.

No mention of a democratic authority is made in the text. This option should **not** be chosen.

'... to support the successful reintegration of the excluded pupil.'

(paragraph 2) is closest in meaning to:

Option A: to maintain the continuing education of the excluded pupil.

This means that while the pupil's education continues they will remain excluded and not integrated within the school. This is not what is meant by the phrase from the passage and this option should **not** be chosen.

Option B: to make the pupil's return to school as constructive as possible.

This means that the pupil should be helped to return and remain in school. **This option should be chosen.**

Option C: to give positive guidance on how to control their behaviour in school.

While this might be one of the supporting measures required, in itself it does not mean reintegration. This option should **not** be chosen.

Option D: to help the pupil settle successfully into their new school.

This option means integration into another school, rather than a return to the school where the problems arose, i.e. reintegration. This option should **not** be chosen.

$\frac{8}{10}$ $\frac{6}{15}$, $\frac{3}{5}$ $\frac{6}{6}$,

$\frac{10}{10}$ $\frac{15}{15}$, $\frac{3}{5}$ $\frac{6}{6}$,

$\frac{}{11}$

$\frac{3}{5}$, $\frac{2}{4}$, $\frac{3}{3}$

$\frac{}{12}$

$\begin{array}{r} 8 \\ 6 \\ 9 \\ + 8 \\ \hline 31 \\ \hline 48 \end{array}$

$\begin{array}{r} 10 \\ 15 \\ 11 \\ + 12 \\ \hline 48 \\ 48 \end{array}$

100% = 48

24

Further reading

Amis, K. (1997) *The King's English*. Harmondsworth: Penguin Books.

Bryson, B. (1986) *Troublesome Words*. Harmondsworth: Penguin Books.

Crystal, D. (2004) *Rediscover Grammar*. Harlow: Longman.

DfES (2000) *Grammar for Writing*. London: DCSF Publications Centre.

Greenbaum, S. (1996) *The Oxford English Grammar*. Oxford: OUP.

Heffer, S. (2010) *Strictly English*. London: Windmill Books.

Medwell, J., Wray, D., Moore, G. and Griffiths, V. (2012) *Primary English – Knowledge and Understanding*, 6th edition. Exeter: Learning Matters.

Trask, R.L. (1997) *The Penguin Guide to Punctuation*. Harmondsworth: Penguin Books.

Truss, L. (2003) *Eats, Shoots and Leaves*. London: Profile Books.

Glossary

*Abbreviation A shortened form of a word or phrase; usually, but not always, consisting of a letter or group of letters taken from the word or phrase. For example, the word *approximately* can be replaced by the abbreviation 'approx'.

Accent An accent is the distinctive system of pronunciation that listeners identify as being used by a regional or social group. Accents are neither easy nor hard to follow, merely familiar or unfamiliar.

*Acronym An abbreviation made from the initial letters of a group of words and often pronounced as a single word, for example, RAM (random access memory).

Adjective An adjective is a word, phrase or clause that tells us about a noun: *clever child*, *tense student*, *concerned teacher*; *a lesson about Spain*; *the teacher who had done supply work there previously*. The clause comes after the noun whereas the phrase may come before (*the predictably over-anxious child from Ashton*) as well as more typically, afterwards.

Adverb Adverbs tell us when, where or how something took place. They usually modify verbs but can also modify adjectives, other adverbs or sentences: *Joe sang happily*; *Annie is a very engaged reader*; *Alice danced very gracefully*; *Lucy had, fortunately, brought her trumpet with her*.

Not all adverbs end in *ly*. *Fast* is usually used as an adverb. *Very*, used above, is an adverb that appears only as an intensifier of some other word.

Adverbial clause An adverbial clause does the work of an adverb: it tells us when, where or how something took place: *The head came into the hall when all the children were there*; *Ann did her print-making where she usually worked*; *Pam ran down the corridor as if she was being chased*.

Adverbial phrase An adverbial phrase also does the work of an adverb. It is a group of words based on an adverb but coming before or after it or both: *very quickly*, *talked as volubly as the deputy*. An adverb can be substituted for an adverbial phrase.

Agree/agreement If one person does something, the verb should be in its singular form: *Annie sings*. If more than one does something, the verb should be in its plural form: *Joe and Sally are painting*.

*Analogy Drawing a comparison to show a similarity; for example, if you were describing the flow of electricity, you might choose to use the flow of water as an analogy.

*Apostrophe A **punctuation mark** used for two purposes:

- to show that something belongs to someone (the *possessive* form); for example, *the pupil's work*, or
- to show that letters have been missed out (a *contraction*); for example, *you've* is the shortened form of *you have*.

Attachment ambiguity Ambiguity may arise when it is unclear if a phrase should be attached to this or that other phrase. In *The teacher told the class what had happened to the caretaker on the stairs*, it is possible to understand that *on the stairs* was where something happened to the caretaker but also that it was *on the stairs* that the teacher told the class.

*Audio Of, or relating to, sound.

Brackets: see **punctuation: parentheses.**

British English This term is normally used to describe the features common to English English, Welsh English, Scottish English, and Hiberno-English.

Bullet points Bullets should only be used to aid comprehension by highlighting key points and breaking up long passages of text. Overuse can be distracting and make text harder to digest. Ideally bullet points should lead out from a 'platform' or 'stem' statement and complete a grammatically correct sentence. However, there are no hard and fast rules on this. Often what is acceptable is governed by a preferred 'house-style'.

Capital letters: see **punctuation.** Use capitals for proper nouns, acronyms and the beginning of sentences. Note that upper case in an acronym does not necessarily denote upper case in the full description, e.g. EPQ/extended project qualification; PGCE/post-graduate certificate in education.

Clause A group of words with a finite verb (it would be a phrase if it did not have a finite verb). As it is finite, the verb typically has a subject. A clause may be a sentence: *Alice laughed.* A sentence may contain several clauses: *Alice laughed and Lucy giggled* links two clauses of equal significance with the conjunction *and*; this is a co-ordinate sentence. *Alice laughed because Lucy giggled* links two clauses that differ in significance; this is a complex sentence in which a main clause – *Alice laughed* – is linked to a subordinate clause that is not independent of other clauses but exists to explain the main clause on which it depends.

Coherence/cohesion A well-made text feels coherent. What holds it together is the writer's use of cohesion: cohesive devices that relate parts of the text to each other. Adverbs between sentences are such devices: *The IT suite was heavily used.* *However, rising numbers were putting pressure on its use.*

Repetition of a word or some reference to it is another device. Perhaps the one we are most aware of is the use of a pronoun to refer to its noun. A noun may refer back to its noun: *The Ofsted report was scrutinised by the Governors before **it** was presented to parents. Although **some** were apprehensive, most of the class looked forward to the cliff-walk.*

*Colloquial A colloquialism is a term used in everyday language rather than in formal speech or writing; for example, the use of the word *kids* rather than *children* in the following sentence:

The kids in Years 4 and 5 are having a swimming gala next week.

*Colon: see **punctuation**.

*Comma: see **punctuation**.

*Compound word A word made when two words are joined to form a new word; for example, *foot/ball*, *foot/fall*. Sometimes, a hyphen is used between the two parts of the word, as in *over-anxious*.

*Conjunctions (see also connectives) These are words such as *and*, *but* and *or*, that are used to join words, phrases or clauses. There are two kinds of conjunction:

– **Co-ordinating conjunctions** (*and*, *but*, *or* and so).These link items that have equal status grammatically, for example:

   *We could fly to Paris **or** we could take the train.*
   *He plans to fly to Dublin **but** he will arrive there very early.*

– **Subordinating conjunctions** (*when, while, before, after, since, until, if, because, although, that*). If the two items do not have equal status, a subordinating conjunction is used. Most commonly, this happens when a main clause is joined to a subordinate clause, for example:
– *I was late for the meeting **because** the train was delayed.*

Connective Connectives connect words, phrases, clauses and sentences. Those that operate *within* the sentence, that connect words, phrases and clauses, are called conjunctions: *and, but, if, or, because, although*, etc. Those that connect sentences (*Pam and Tom worked very hard all term. **Luckily,** their efforts paid off*) include some conjunctions but also adverbs such as: *On the other hand, Later, While we were singing*, etc.

Consistency A good style is, among other things, consistent. The writer will always spell *judgement* with that first *e* or always without it. Punctuation demands a very consistent style, as when adverbs such as *however* always appear between commas if they occur in the middle of a sentence.

*Consonant Consonants are letters and speech sounds that are not vowels. See **vowel**.

Contraction If we try to write down informal speech, we will sometimes need contractions. These help us to write some contracted combinations of words: *do not* becomes *don't, will not* becomes *won't*. The words are contracted by omitting some letters and inserting an apostrophe into the space that is left. Occasionally, as with *won't*, there is also a change in spelling.

*Contradict, contradicted, contradiction To contradict is to state that something is the opposite of what has been said; a contradiction is a statement that contradicts.

Convention While the rules of grammar, like the laws of gravity, get their authority by describing how things are, there are some practices that are matters of social convention and have no other explanation. The conventions governing spelling and punctuation, for example, have changed over time.

*Dash Use a dash, rather than a hyphen, to represent ranges of numbers, e.g. 11–16 years.

A pair of dashes can be used to separate an interruption within a sentence, e.g. 'Most pupils – especially in extended schools – enjoy after school activities'. If the interruption comes at the end of the sentence, only one dash is used.

*Definite article The; see **determiner**.

*Department for Education In full at first mention, then the DfE.

*Determiner These are words used with nouns to help define them, for example, *this computer*, *a pencil*, *the book*, and limit, i.e. determine the reference of the noun in some way. Determiners include:

- articles (*a/an*, *the*)
- demonstratives (*this/that*, *these/those*)
- possessives (*my/your/his/her/its/our/their*)
- quantifiers (*some*, *any*, *no*, *many*, *few*, *all*, *either*, *each*, etc.)
- numbers (*one*, *two*, *three*, etc.), and
- some question words (*which*, *what*, *whose*).

Words that are used as determiners are followed by a noun (though not necessarily immediately). For example, *this* book is yours; *this* black book is yours; *which* book is yours?

Many determiners can also be used as **pronouns**. These include demonstrative pronouns, question words, numbers and most quantifiers. When used as pronouns, determiners are not followed by a noun; they refer to the noun: *this is for you* (where *this* refers to *this school*, *this book*, etc.).

Dialect A variety of a language that is spoken by a specific group or in a specific area of the country and whose words and grammar show some differences from those used in other dialects of English. The prestige of a dialect derives from the prestige of its speakers, not from its linguistic features. *Accent* is usually taken to be related but different because it focuses on the *substance* of the language: in the case of an accent, that substance is the sound of speech.

*Dialogue A conversation between two or more people.

Digraph Two letters that represent one sound: *ch* and *ck* in *check*; *sh* in *show*; *ph* in *phonically*.

*Discourse marker A word or phrase (such as *however*, *nevertheless*, *well*, *OK*, or *right!*) that is used to signal a pause or change of direction in conversation.

Ellipsis If a sentence can be understood when a word or a group of words is removed, the parts deleted have been ellipted. One of the commonest examples of ellipsis is the dropping of the relative pronoun *that*: *The school [that] I like best*. A more sophisticated usage is: *My class, if lively, is still well behaved*. *If lively* here is an ellipted version of something like *even if it is lively*.

*Evaluate To assess; when asked to evaluate whether a statement is supported or implied by a text, you are being asked to judge how clearly the text does or does not spell out the information given in the statement.

*Fewer/less Use 'fewer' for things you can count (e.g. books, pupils) and 'less' for things you can't count (e.g. space, scope).

Grammar Grammar, or syntax, is usually used to mean how sentences are organised. It can, however, also refer to the organisation of larger units: the text level. *Cohesion* is the study of the grammar of these larger units. *Morphology* is the branch of grammar that deals with word-formation.

*Hyphens Use hyphens for compound adjectives, e.g. the up-to-date situation but keep the directory up to date, a long-term plan but in the long term. Do not use a hyphen between an adverb and the adjective or the verb it modifies, e.g. a hotly disputed penalty, a constantly evolving policy.

*Imply, implied, implicit Something implied is hinted at without being stated explicitly. It is implicit.

*Indefinite article *A* or *an*; see **determiner**.

Infinitive The (non-finite) form of a verb that opens with *to*: *to learn, to study, to think.*

Morpheme The smallest bit of language that has meaning. A morpheme may be a whole word (*cabbage*) or a word may have several morphemes (*un + help + ful, govern + or, head + teach + er*). **Suffixes** and **prefixes** are all morphemes.

Morphology see **grammar**.

Noun Nouns refer to objects, ideas, things, places. They take a plural form (usually, add *s*).

Some nouns, however, do not normally take a plural form: *happiness*. They have a possessive form (add *'s* or *s'*). They can be substituted by a pronoun, take a word like *the, this, a* before them and take a verb after them.

- **Noun phrase:** a group of words that works as a noun. A pronoun could be substituted for it: *The first person to have been Chair of the Education Committee.*
- **Noun clause:** a group of words that has a finite verb and that acts as a noun. Here, the clause acts as the subject: ***That I was late with my reports yet again*** was hard to swallow. Here, it acts as the object: *The class was desperate to know **if the school trip was still on**.*
- **Collective nouns** refer to a group of things or people: *collection, family, group, class, set.* It is usually safest to treat collective nouns as singular unless the meaning is that they should be read as plural.
- **Proper nouns** refer to specific people, places, organisations, etc., and have a capital initial letter: *Dot, Mike; Salford, Canterbury; Training and Development Agency.*

Paragraph One or more sentences grouped together because they are about the same topic or because they form one utterance in a dialogue. It is separated from the adjacent paragraphs by beginning on a new line.

Parenthesis A word or phrase that interrupts the sentence is marked at both boundaries by parentheses: brackets, commas or dashes:

The Irwell (which flows through Salford) was the focus of their local studies.
The Irwell – which flows through Salford – was the focus of their local studies.
The Irwell, which flows through Salford, was the focus of their local studies.

Participle The present participle is a form of the verb that ends in *ing*: *learning, reading, writing*; the past participle is a form of the verb that ends, normally, in *ed*: *talked, walked, displayed*. However, there are irregular verbs that have other endings: *bought, written, sung*, etc.

The present participle is used to construct continuous tenses: *she was teaching, she is teaching, she will be teaching*. It sometimes works as a noun (it can then be called a gerund): *learning is good*.

The past participle follows an auxiliary verb to form the perfect past tense: *I have taught, they have learned*. The passive voice uses an auxiliary with a past participle: *the class was cheated out of their expected success, the in-service day was cancelled*.

Both participles can be used as adjectives: *broken, breaking, entangled*.

Phoneme A single speech sound. We use 44–48 different phonemes when we speak English, depending on the accent we use. Spelling tries to represent phonemes but tries to do other things as well that may conflict with that attempt. The letters *th* in *this* represent one phoneme but in *thing* they represent a different phoneme.

Phonetics Phonetics is a way of describing the sounds we use in speech. It has nothing to do with phonics.

Phrase A group of words without a verb (it would be a clause if it had a finite verb). Phrases can be **nouns**: *the twentieth position in the class*; **adjectives**: *very clever*; **adverbs**: *too early*; or **verbs**: *was practising*.

Plural The plural form of a noun shows that more than one thing is being referred to. Plural nouns typically end in *s* (*book + s = books*; *girl + s = girls*), *es* (*box + es = boxes, circus + es = circuses*) or *ies* (*fairy* becomes *fairies, story* becomes *stories*). There are also some irregular plurals, such as *children, women, men, geese, sheep*.

Possessive Possessive pronouns – *my/mine*, etc. – show who or what owns what: *my whiteboard, its cursor*. In writing, nouns show possession by adding an apostrophe and, as appropriate, the letter *s*.

Predicate The part of a sentence that is not the subject; it is about the subject: *The headteacher arrived too early.*

Prefix A **morpheme** that is added at the beginning of a word: *a* in *atheist,* *un* in *unhelpful.*

Preposition Prepositions usually link a noun or noun phrase with another one or with a verb. Prepositions such as *at, on, in, over, by, with, near, through* are used to introduce adjective phrases in *The display **over** the radiator* or *That boy **by** the boundary fence* and to introduce adverb phrases in *Joe is **on** the go as usual* and *Annie's balloon rose **into** the sky.*

Pronoun A word used instead of a noun, a noun phrase or a group of nouns. It may be a **personal pronoun**: *I/me, you/you, he/him, she/her, it/it, we/us, they/them*; a **possessive pronoun**: *my/mine, your/yours, his/his, her/hers, our/ours, their/theirs, its/its*; a **reflexive pronoun**: *myself, herself, themselves*; or an **interrogative pronoun** (used in questions): *who/whom, whose, which, what.*

Punctuation The standard set of marks used in written and printed texts to clarify meaning and to separate sentences, words and parts of words. The most commonly used punctuation marks in English are:

- **apostrophe** (')
- **colon** (:)
- **comma** (,)
- **exclamation mark** (!)
- **full stop** (.)
- **hyphen** (-)
- **inverted commas** (see *speech marks*)
- **parentheses** (singular: *parenthesis,* also known as brackets or ellipses (singular, ellipsis) (())
- **semi-colon** (;)
- **speech marks,** also known as quotation marks or inverted commas (" " or ' ')
- **question mark** (?).

Also included are special signals such as:

- the use of a space before and after a block or words to indicate the start of a new paragraph
- the convention of using an upper case (or capital) letter to begin a proper name or a new sentence.

*Redundancy Redundancy is the use of duplicative, unnecessary or useless wording, also known as **tautology.**

Relative clause Relative clauses come after nouns and function as adjectives. Typically, they open with a relative pronoun: *who, whom, that, which, whose: The teacher **that we hoped to appoint** was not as experienced as two other candidates.* Note that, in this case, the relative pronoun, *that,* can be deleted without losing the meaning.

Sentence A sentence is a clause or a group of clauses. Each clause needs to have a finite verb.

- **Finite verbs** are ones that tell us about tense; they almost invariably have a subject: *Ann and Tony both found maths easy.*
- **Non-finite verb** forms are the infinitive – *to teach* – and the participles that end in *-ed* or *-ing*.
- **Sentences can be declarative:** *The class rushed into the hall*; **interrogative:** *Can't your class do anything quietly?*; **imperative:** *Slow Down!* or **exclamative:** *That's great!*

*Sentence stem In the test items, this is the first part of a sentence that requires completion by choosing from several possible endings, for example:

There were four kinds of meetings that day: ... followed by a list.

Singular Nouns can be singular or plural: *book* or *books*; *woman* or *women*. Verbs can also show singularity – *I teach, she teaches* – or plurality – *we teach, they teach.*

STA The Standards and Testing Agency is an executive agency of the Department for Education. The STA is responsible for the development and delivery of all statutory assessments from Early Years to the end of Key Stage 3. This work was previously carried out by the Qualifications and Curriculum Development Agency.

*Standard English The variety of English used in public communication, particularly in writing.

*Statement A sentence that contains a fact or proposition, for example, *this is a glossary.*

Subject A sentence has a subject (a noun or a pronoun) that does something (the verb): ***She*** *taught sentence structure very clearly.*

Suffix A **morpheme** that is added at the end of a word: *ed* in *walked, ful* in *helpful.*

Syntax Grammar: how sentences are organised.

Tautology The unnecessary repetition of the same idea in different words: in *The Governors met together*, the last word is unnecessary.

*Unit of meaning An identifiably discrete idea.

Verb Words that say what we do or are: *The teacher **stopped** the class because one child **was being** silly.*

- **Active verbs** (verbs in the active voice) tell us what someone did: *Lucy **thanked** the teacher.* **Passive verbs** (verbs in the passive voice) tell us what was done to somebody: *The teacher was **thanked** by Lucy.*
- **Auxiliary verbs** – the main ones are *be, have, do* – accompany main verbs to show tense: *They **have** painted, they **do** run.* Some, called **modal verbs**, express possibility or obligation: *can, could, may, might, will, would, shall, should, must, ought to.*

- **Tense** is the way that a verb tells us when something happened. This is shown in the different forms of the verb, from the past – *learned, has learned, had learned* – to the present – *learns, is learning, does learn* – to the future – *will learn, will have learned*, etc.
- **Number** is the way that a verb shows if one or more than one **subject** did something: *Alice sings, Annie and Joe sing*.

*Vowel The letters a, e, i, o, u; see also **consonant**.

Note

Entries marked with * have been reproduced by courtesy of the TA © Teaching Agency. Permission to reproduce TA copyright material does not extend to any material that is identified as being the copyright of a third party nor to any photographs.